Soft Furnishings with your OVERLOCKER

A step-by-step creative guide to over fifty projects

•LINETTE MARITZ•

NEW HOLLAND

First published in the UK in 1993 by
New Holland (Publishers) Ltd
37 Connaught Street
London W2 2AZ

ISBN 1 85368 253 5

Editor: Marie Gerber
Designer: Tracey Carstens
Cover design: Tracey Carstens
Photographer: Derek Williams
Stylist: Marine Williams
Colour illustrations: Nicci Page
Line drawings: Jacques le Roux

Typeset by BellSet
Reproduction by Unifoto (Pty) Ltd
Printed and bound in Singapore by Tien Wah Press (Pte) Ltd

CONTENTS

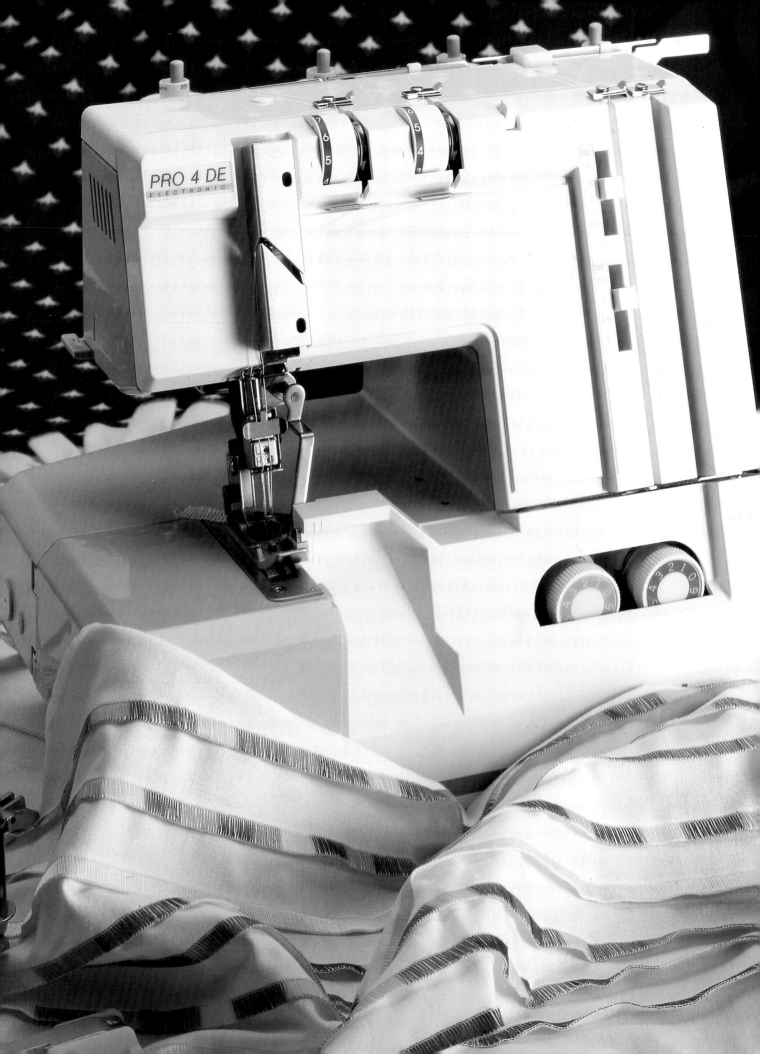

INTRODUCTION

Overlockers have taken the market by storm. Used in conjunction with a sewing machine, they save time and money and help you to create articles with a personal touch. However, unless you understand how an overlocker operates, it cannot be utilised to its fullest potential.

An overlocker sews, overlocks and neatens the edge in one operation at approximately 1 500 stitches per minute. An overlocker cannot be used to make buttonholes or to insert a zip and, except in the case of a five-thread overlocker, it cannot be used for straight stitching. But it can be used for sewing, overlocking, edging, gathering, hemming, decorating and much, much more, as you will discover.

At first glance, all overlockers may look similar, but on closer inspection it becomes clear that, although they are all used to neaten edges, there are vast differences between the models and makes of overlocker on the market.

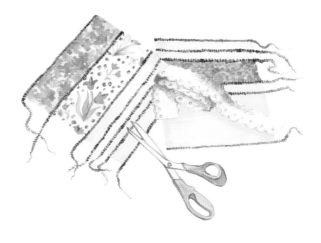

NEEDLES

Needles form a very important part of any overlocker and great care should be taken when changing and selecting the various needles.

Lock needles (suitable for your make and model of overlocker)   size 80/90
Universal needles   size 80/90
Ballpoint needles   size 80/90

- A denim or leather needle cannot be used on an overlocker as the eye of the needle is shaped differently and will hit the loopers when sewing.
- Always use two similar needles, for example two ballpoint needles or two lock needles.
- Always use two needles of a similar size, for example two size 80 needles.

> NOTE: When one needle breaks, replace both needles. This will ensure that you are always using two needles of similar type and size.

- On a four-thread safety stitch overlocker, the right needle is always situated slightly lower than the left needle. If both needles are positioned at the same height, the timing of the needles will be inaccurate in relation to the loopers and the machine will skip stitches and not form the stitches correctly.
- On a four- or five-thread overlocker with a chain stitch, the front needle is always situated lower than the back needle. If both needles are positioned at the same height, the overlocker will skip stitches.
- When replacing a needle, ensure that the flat side of the needle is turned towards the back and the round side towards the front of the overlocker.

> NOTE: Never abuse your overlocker, as it can only respond when operated correctly. Do not let anyone else use your overlocker unless you or the dealer from whom you purchased your machine has shown that person how to use it correctly.

- When replacing a needle, be sure to push the needle up as high as possible before tightening the clamp screw with a screwdriver or an Allen key.
- Change the needles regularly to ensure trouble-free sewing. Replace lock needles after every six to eight hours of sewing, and universal and ballpoint needles after every four to six hours.

THREADS

- Always use good quality polyester cotton thread on your overlocker.
- Polyester cotton thread combinations consist of cotton-wrapped polyester strands. The cotton sheath provides heat resistance and gives the thread the appearance of cotton, while the polyester core provides strength and elasticity. Polyester cotton thread is well suited for use on an overlocker because, as the machine sews at high speeds (at a rate of 1 500 stitches per minute), the thread must be able to stretch, irrespective of the type of fabric used.

> NOTE: If you find that the polyester cotton thread keeps snapping even though the tension is set correctly, it is probably because the cotton is dry due to exposure to sunlight. Place the reels in an empty container and leave in the refrigerator for a day or two. The cotton will absorb the moisture and regain its elasticity. This procedure can be repeated every six months.

- Always ensure that the different reels of polyester cotton thread you are using on your overlocker are all the same brand so as to avoid adjusting the tension frequently.
- When buying polyester cotton thread, buy reels of 1 000 m or 5 000 m as these not only give better value for money, but also unwind more evenly. The cotton on smaller reels (100 m or 200 m) often snaps because the overlocker operates at such high speed.
- Floss or bulk nylon can only be used on the loopers.
- Floss consists of strands of polyester and/or nylon fibres. Depending on the quantities used by the manufacturers, it

> NOTE: Always use spool caps when sewing with polyester cotton thread. These will ensure that the reel unwinds evenly which, in turn, will ensure a more even tension.

could contain more polyester or more nylon. Bulk nylon is available from most sewing machine stockists. Some manufacturers refer to it as floss, for example DMC and Metler.

- On a four-thread overlocker, four reels of polyester cotton thread or two reels of polyester cotton thread and two reels of floss may be used.
- On a five-thread overlocker, five reels of polyester cotton thread or three reels of polyester cotton thread and two reels of floss may be used.

TENSION

When threading your overlocker, keep the thread pulled tightly to ensure that it is properly inserted into the tension spring on the tension knob. If the thread is not inserted properly, the overlocking stitch will form loops on the front of the article.

The tension settings on a four-thread overlocker are as follows:

LEFT NEEDLE

This is the outside needle. Of the four tension settings on your overlocker, the tension setting for this needle must always be the highest, as this controls the thread which holds the seam together and prevents it from pulling open.

RIGHT NEEDLE

This is the inside needle and is also known as the mock safety stitch. The tension setting for this needle must always be lower than that of the outside needle, as this controls the thread which supports the outside thread. If the tension is set too high, the seam will pucker.

UPPER LOOPER

This needle controls the thread which lies across on top of the stitching. The tension setting must always be as low as possible to prevent the seam from pulling open.

LOWER LOOPER

This needle controls the thread which lies across the bottom of the stitching. The tension setting must always be as low as possible to prevent the seam from pulling open.

> NOTE: On an overlocker, 0 signals a very low setting and 9 a very high tension setting.

STITCH LENGTH

The stitch length is the distance between the stitches and the loops formed. The desired stitch length will depend on the thickness of the fabric and the finish required. A short stitch length is used on thin fabrics, for example silk or viscose, as it prevents the fabric from puckering, and for sewing a narrow hem. A long stitch length is suitable for heavier or thicker fabrics, for example denim or wadding (batting), and for gathering.

PRESSURE KNOB

The pressure knob is used to increase or decrease the pressure of the sewing foot on the fabric. For thin fabrics, increase the pressure to prevent puckering. For thick fabrics, decrease the pressure to prevent the fabric from bunching and knits from stretching.

MOVING AND FIXED BLADE

There are two blades on an overlocker which will cut the edge of the fabric before it is overlocked.

Moving blade: Depending on the make and model of your overlocker, this blade is usually made of strong steel and will not have to be replaced. On some models the moving blade can be locked when sewing thick fabrics or disengaged for decorative sewing.

Fixed blade: Depending on the make and model of your overlocker, this blade is usually made of soft steel and must be replaced when it no longer cuts cleanly and leaves edges frayed. The fixed blade controls the cutting width, which can be adjusted, depending on the type of fabric used.

DIFFERENTIAL FEED

Most overlockers are equipped with a differential feed for perfect fabric control. This means that the overlocker has two sets of 'feed dogs'. The purpose of the feed dog is to feed the fabric through from the bottom. The speed of the feed dog can be controlled by adjusting the differential feed knob.

When the differential feed knob is set on 0.5 – 0.7, the front feed dog is set to feed the fabric through at a slower speed to prevent thin fabrics, such as silk, viscose or net, from puckering.

When the differential feed knob is set on 1.0, the front and back feed dogs feed the fabric through at the same speed. This is the normal setting and is used when sewing cotton, polyester cotton, linen or tracksuiting.

When the differential feed knob is set on 1.5, the front feed dog will feed the fabric through faster than the back feed dog. This setting, therefore, is suitable for thicker fabrics, such as woven tracksuiting and can also be used to facilitate sewing when joining seams or sewing over seams.

When the differential feed knob is set on 2.0, the front feed dog will feed the fabric through faster than at a setting of 1.5 and prevents knits from waving or stretching. It also prevents thick fabrics from bunching up. Use this setting when sewing very thick fabrics such as denim or leather, when applying rib trim, sewing wadding, or covering shoulder pads.

This setting can also be used to gather fabrics, as described under DECORATIVE TECHNIQUES USING THE OVERLOCKER on page 11.

OVERLOCKING STITCHES

The overlocking stitch is formed around a stitch tongue with the use of loopers and needles. The type of stitching depends on the number of needles and loopers used.

THREE-THREAD OVERLOCKING

This stitch is formed around the stitch tongue with the use of one needle and two loopers. This is the most basic stitch formed on an overlocker. The three-thread stitch can be used on its own if, for example, it is used for a seam that is not under stress, such as when joining two frills. The stitch can also be used in conjunction with a sewing machine to finish an edge.

All decorative finishing, for example flatlocking, faggoting and narrow hemming (see pages 11 – 18), is always done with three threads.

FOUR-THREAD OVERLOCKING

This stitch is formed around the stitch tongue with the use of two needles and two loopers. This stitch is also known as the mock safety stitch.

The four-thread stitch is 6 – 7 mm (approximately ¼ in) wide and is used for seams. This stitch is particularly suitable for stretch fabrics. The overlocker can also be converted to a three-thread stitch by removing the left needle to form a narrow stitch, or by removing the right needle to form a wide stitch.

FOUR-THREAD OVERLOCKING (CHAIN AND OVERLOCKING)

This stitch is a combination of a chain stitch and two-thread overlocking. All four threads must be used to sew a seam. The chain stitch cannot be used on its own, and two-thread overlocking is not strong enough to hold the seam. This stitch is suitable for woven fabrics, as the chain stitch does not stretch.

FIVE-THREAD OVERLOCKING

The five-thread overlocker has many possibilities as it operates with two needles and three loopers. On some models, the five-thread overlocker can also be used as a four-thread overlocker by changing the needles, or by inserting a special double needle to obtain a mock safety stitch finish suitable for sewing stretch fabrics. It also forms a two-thread chain stitch which functions as a conventional straight stitch and is mainly used for decorative purposes. Five-thread overlocking is suitable for woven fabrics.

OVERLOCKER ACCESSORIES

Consult your dealer or agent for more information about the different accessories, feet and attachments available for your particular make and model of overlocker.

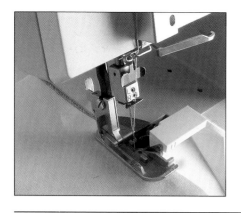

ROLLED HEM PLATE OR ATTACHMENT

This is a standard accessory supplied with all three-, four- or five-thread overlockers. It can form an integral part of the overlocker, or be a plate or attachment which can be fitted onto the machine. This plate or attachment produces a narrow stitch, as the stitches are formed around a narrower stitch tongue, which is ideal for sewing narrow or rolled hems.

A narrow hem gives a decorative finish to linen, polyester, cotton and viscose. The fabric is rolled while the stitches are being formed, but the tension locks at the edge of the fabric.

A rolled hem is very narrow and is used on net, organza and thin, silky fabrics. Used with gut, on wedding dresses for example, it gives a scalloped edge. When the stitches are formed, the fabric as well as the tension roll over and lock at the back.

ELASTIC GATHERER ATTACHMENT OR FOOT

This optional attachment or foot can be fitted onto a three-, four- or five-thread overlocker and is used to gather elastic and sew it onto the fabric in one operation, or to sew on cord or ribbon using three-thread overlocking.

1. Attach or clip the elastic gatherer attachment or foot onto your overlocker. To attach the elastic, thread the elastic through under the attachment or foot and, depending on the width of the elastic you are using, use either the right or the left needle.

2. To sew on cord or ribbon, thread it through the hole in the attachment or foot and, depending on the width of the ribbon or cord, use either the left or the right needle when sewing over ribbon and the right needle when sewing over cord.

NEEDLE	THREAD	TENSION
Left/right needle	polyester cotton thread	balanced
Upper looper	polyester cotton thread or floss	balanced
Lower looper	polyester cotton thread or floss	balanced

Stitch length: 3 – 3½
Differential feed: 1.0
• The moving blade must be in the cutting position.

BLIND HEM ATTACHMENT OR FOOT

This optional attachment or foot can be fitted onto a three-, four- or five-thread overlocker. It enables you to cut and overlock while hemming, using three-thread overlocking. Depending on the make and model of overlocker, use the right or left needle. Test this accessory on a scrap of fabric before sewing and adjust the cloth guide of the foot so that the needle only catches one or two fibres on the fold.

1. Attach or clip the blind hem attachment or foot onto the overlocker. Fold the hem back the desired width to the wrong side and then fold it back towards the right side of the article, leaving a 1 cm (½ in) raw edge.

2. Place the fabric under the blind hem attachment or foot, with the folded edge on top against the guide and sew, using three-thread overlocking.

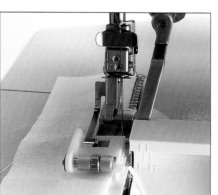

NEEDLE	THREAD	TENSION
Left/right needle	polyester cotton thread	2 – 3 (loosen)
Upper looper	polyester cotton thread or floss	balanced
Lower looper	polyester cotton thread or floss	balanced

Stitch length: 3 – 3½
Differential feed: 1.0
• The moving blade must be in the cutting position.

GATHERING ATTACHMENT OR FOOT

This attachment or foot is an optional accessory which fits onto a three-, four- or five-thread overlocker. This accessory enables you to gather the fabric on the bottom while sewing it onto the fabric on top.

The length of the fabric to be gathered should be approximately 1½ – 2 times the length of the fabric to which it is to be gathered. The number of gathers will depend on the thickness of the fabric. If this accessory is used in conjunction with the differential feed, the fabric will have more gathers.

For instructions on how to use the gathering attachment or foot, refer to the section on DECORATIVE TECHNIQUES USING THE OVERLOCKER (see pages 11 – 18).

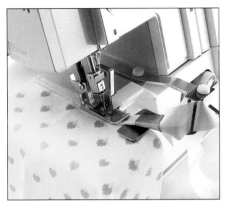

TAPE GUIDE

PIPING FOOT

TAPE GUIDE

The tape guide is an optional accessory which fits onto a three-, four- or five-thread overlocker and can be used separately or in conjunction with the piping foot. The tape guide folds the pre-cut tape over and sews it in between two layers of fabric. If used in conjunction with the piping foot, nylon cord can be fed through the tape guide so that piping can be made and sewn onto the fabric in one operation.

1. Attach the tape guide and feed 2.5 cm-wide (1 in-wide) pre-cut strips of fabric into the tape guide, and underneath the foot. Sew on tape using three-thread overlocking.

NEEDLE	THREAD	TENSION
Left needle	polyester cotton thread	balanced
Upper looper	polyester cotton thread	balanced
Lower looper	polyester cotton thread	balanced

Stitch length: 2 ½ – 3
Differential feed: Depends on the thickness and number of layers of fabric
• The moving blade must be in the cutting position.

PIPING FOOT

The piping foot is used in conjunction with the tape guide to make your own piping and sew it onto the fabric all in one operation. This optional accessory can be fitted onto a three-, four- or five-thread overlocker. With a four-thread overlocker, the left or right needle can be used, depending on the make and model of your overlocker.

Clip or attach the foot onto your overlocker and use with tape guide.

BIAS BINDER WITH CHAIN STITCH

The bias binder can only be fitted onto a five-thread overlocker. The chain stitch is used with the bias binder.

1. Cut the bias strips to measure (see page 10).

2. Attach the bias binder to the front of the overlocker and feed the pre-cut bias strips through the bias binder and underneath the foot.

3. Adjust the bias binder so that the chain stitch is sewn onto the edge where the bias binding has been folded.

4. Place the fabric in the bias binder, ensuring that the fabric is encased in the bias strip.

NEEDLE	THREAD	TENSION
Chain needle	polyester cotton thread	balanced
Chain looper	polyester cotton thread	balanced

Stitch length: 3 – 4
Differential feed: Depends on the thickness of the fabric

TO MAKE YOUR OWN BIAS BINDING

1. Cut a rectangle of fabric measuring 70 cm x 35 cm (27½ in x 13¾ in). This should be sufficient for a bias strip of 3 m (3¼ yd).

2. Fold one corner of the fabric to a 45 degree angle and, using a marking pen, draw a line on the fold (see Fig. 1).

Fig. 1

3. Draw lines parallel to the first line, approximately 4 cm (1½ in) apart, until the far corner is reached.

4. Mark the lines A to F as shown (see Fig. 2).

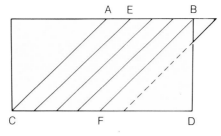

Fig. 2

5. Cut out the parallelogram as shown (see Fig. 3).

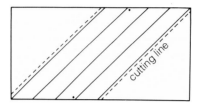

Fig. 3

6. To join the lines, take corner C to point E and turn the fabric to form a V 1 cm (½ in) from the raw edge. Pin.

7. Bring corner B to point F to form a V 1 cm (½ in) from the raw edge.

8. Using the sewing machine and straight stitch, sew 1 cm (½ in) from the raw edge on the pinned Vs (see Fig. 4).

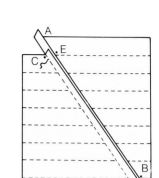

Fig. 4

9. Press seam.

10. Starting at one uneven end, cut along the marked lines to form one continuous strip of bias binding.

TO FINISH OFF SEAMS

To prevent the unsecured threads from coming undone, use one of the following methods.

Chaining off: Chain (continue sewing) off the edge of the fabric for a short distance. Pull the needle threads tightly and knot (see Fig. 5). Cut the ends and apply a dab of stitch sealant (see page 19) to secure the ends. Allow to dry for one minute.

Sewing in a circle: When you begin to sew in a circle, sew diagonally from the raw edge to the stitching line. Continue to sew in a circle, keeping the fabric in a straight line. When returning to the starting point, sew over the diagonal stitches and continue along the sewn edge for a further 2 cm (¾ in). Chain off, pull the needle threads tightly and knot (see Fig. 6). Cut the thread and apply stitch sealant (see page 19) to secure the ends.

Ripping out: To undo the overlocked stitches, cut and pull the needle threads (see Fig. 7). The overlocked edge will come undone. This method will ensure that the seams of an article are all the same width and that there is no unnecessary thickness on the inner seams.

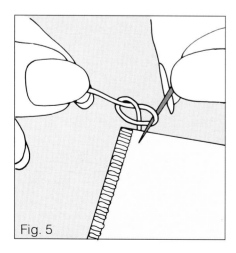

Fig. 5

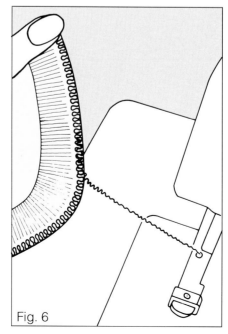

Fig. 6

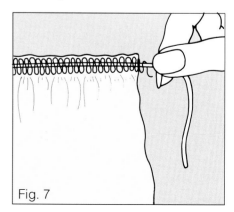

Fig. 7

DECORATIVE TECHNIQUES USING THE OVERLOCKER

FLATLOCKING

Flatlocking is a seam sewn with three threads on two layers of fabric or one layer of fabric and lace. The fabric is then pulled open to obtain a flat decorative seam.

- The width of the flatlocking depends on the width of the lace, the size of the strips or pieces of fabric to be joined, and the size of the article in relation to the decorative stitching. Depending on the width required, the left or the right needle can be used together with both loopers.
- When sewing a flatlocked seam, the needle tension should be set lower while the tension on the lower looper is set higher.
- Flatlocking can be used to join lace onto the edge of a piece of fabric or to sew it on top of the fabric. Use broderie anglaise, nylon or insertion lace which is wide enough to give an effective finish. When sewing flatlocking on fabric and lace, keep the lace at the bottom and the fabric on top.
- A flatlocked seam can either be sewn onto the raw edge of the fabric, or the fabric can be folded double so that the flatlocking is sewn in the centre.
- When joining different colours of fabric, the flatlocking is sewn on the raw edge with the moving blade in the cutting position.
- For a decorative flatlocked seam in the centre of the fabric, disengage the moving blade and while sewing keep the folded edge in line with the edge of the plate.
- When sewing flatlocked seams, the stitching should face downwards or outwards when the seam is pulled open.
- For a decorative flatlocked finish on the right side of the fabric, place the wrong sides of the fabric together before sewing.
- For a decorative ladder stitch on the right side, place the right sides the fabric together.

Interesting effects can be obtained by using different types of thread for a flatlocked decoration. There is no need to keep to the general rule of using the same type of cotton or floss throughout. Let your imagination run riot!

> NOTE: Always sew slowly when working with decorative thread to prevent the thread from snapping or hooking as this could damage the overlocker.

FLATLOCKING WITH FLOSS

1. Place WS of fabric together.
2. Pull the seam open afterwards so that it lies flat.

NEEDLE	THREAD	TENSION
Left/right needle	polyester cotton thread	0 – 2 (loosen)
Upper looper	floss	0 – ½
Lower looper	floss	5 – 7 (tighten)

Stitch length: 2 – 3
Differential feed: Depends on the thickness of the fabric
- The moving blade can be in the cutting position or disengaged.

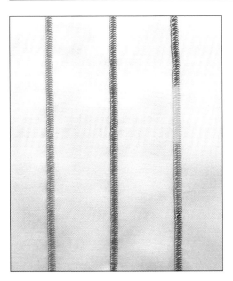

FLATLOCKING WITH METALLIC THREAD

Use good quality, strong metallic threads which are available in plain or variegated shades and can be used to create interesting effects.

Place WS of fabric together and sew. Pull seam open afterwards to lie flat.

NEEDLE	THREAD	TENSION
Left/right needle	polyester cotton thread	0 – 2 (loosen)
Upper looper	metallic thread	1 – 2
Lower looper	polyester cotton thread	5 – 8 (tighten)
	or floss	2 – 5 (tighten)

Stitch length: 1 – 2
Differential feed: Depends on the thickness of the fabric
- The moving blade can be in the cutting position or disengaged.

FLATLOCKING WITH EMBROIDERY THREAD

Use embroidery thread no 8/12, crochet cotton no 8/12, perle cotton no 8/12 or ribbon thread. One- or two-ply wool

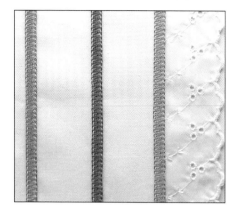

can also be used if it is thin enough to be threaded through the eye of the looper. When sewing with embroidery thread, the upper looper tension must always be set as close as possible to 0 (as low as possible). If the tension has

been set on 0 but is still too tight, then bypass a threading point, in most cases the first threading point.

1. Place WS of fabric together and sew. Pull seam open afterwards to lie flat.

NEEDLE	THREAD	TENSION
Left/right needle	polyester cotton thread	0 – 2 (loosen)
Upper looper	embroidery thread	0 – ½ (loosen)
Lower looper	polyester cotton thread	5 – 8 (tighten)
	or floss	2 – 5 (tighten)

Stitch length: 2 – 3½
Differential feed: Depends on the thickness of the fabric
• The moving blade can be in the cutting position or disengaged.

FLATLOCKING OVER RIBBON WITH METALLIC THREAD OR FLOSS

Use 3 mm-wide (about ⅛ in-wide) satin ribbon when sewing with the right needle, and 5 mm-wide (about ¼ in-wide) satin ribbon if using the left

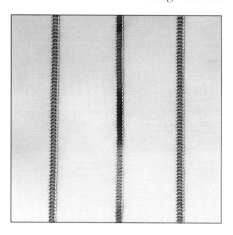

needle. The ribbon must not be wider than the flatlocking.

1. If the ribbon is sewn onto the edge with lace, place the lace at the bottom on the fold of the fabric with the WS of the lace to the RS of the fabric. Place the

ribbon on top, and sew. Keep the ribbon on the inside of the blade so that the edges of the fabric, and not the ribbon, are cut.

2. Pull the seam open afterwards so that it lies flat.

NEEDLE	THREAD	TENSION
Left/right needle	polyester cotton thread	0 – 2 (loosen)
Upper looper	metallic thread	½ – 1
	or floss	0 – ½
Lower looper	polyester cotton thread	5 – 8 (tighten)

Stitch length: 2 – 3
Differential feed: Depends on the thickness of the fabric
• The moving blade can be in the cutting position or disengaged.

LADDER STITCH WITH METALLIC THREAD

The ladder stitch is the wrong side of the flatlocking.

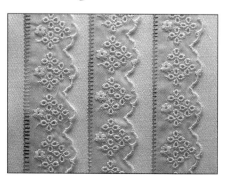

1. Place RS of the fabric or RS fabric and lace together and sew.

2. Pull the seam open afterwards so that it lies flat.

NEEDLE	THREAD	TENSION
Left/right needle	metallic thread	0 – 1 (loosen)
Upper looper	polyester cotton thread	½ – 1
	or floss	0 – ½
Lower looper	polyester cotton thread	5 – 8 (tighten)
	floss	2 – 5 (tighten)

Stitch length: 2 – 2½
Differential feed: Depends on the thickness of the fabric
• The moving blade can be in the cutting position or disengaged.

FLATLOCKED HEM WITH POLYESTER COTTON THREAD, METALLIC THREAD OR FLOSS

Flatlocking can also be used to form a hem. Use the left needle to obtain wide flatlocking and the right needle for narrow flatlocking to ensure that the hem is in proportion to the size of the article. It is important to disengage the moving blade before sewing.

1. Fold the fabric back to the wrong side to the desired hem width, then fold the fabric again so that the raw edge lies inside the fold. Sew on the right side of the fabric on the fold through all the layers, catching the raw edge in the folded edge and keeping the folded edge in line with the edge of the plate.

2. Pull the hem open afterwards to obtain a flat hem.

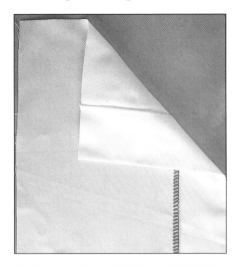

NEEDLE	THREAD	TENSION
Left needle	polyester cotton thread	0 – 2 (loosen)
Upper looper	polyester cotton thread	½ – 1 (loosen)
	metallic thread	0 – 1 (loosen)
	floss	0 – ½ (loosen)
Lower looper	polyester cotton thread	5 – 8 (tighten)
	floss	2 – 5 (tighten)

Stitch length: 2 – 3
Differential feed: Depends on the thickness of the fabric
• The moving blade must be disengaged.

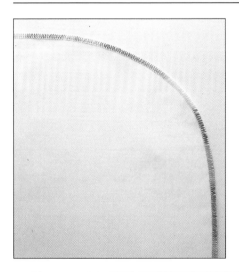

THREE-THREAD OVERLOCKING WITH METALLIC THREAD OR FLOSS

1. Place WS of the fabric together and sew, using three-thread overlocking.

NEEDLE	THREAD	TENSION
Right needle	polyester cotton thread	balanced
Upper looper	metallic thread or floss	balanced
Lower looper	metallic thread or floss	balanced

Stitch length: 1 – 2
Differential feed: Depends on the thickness of the fabric
• The moving blade must be in the cutting position.

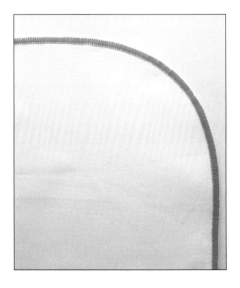

THREE-THREAD WIDE OVERLOCKING WITH METALLIC THREAD OR FLOSS

1. Place WS of the fabric together and sew, using three-thread overlocking.

NEEDLE	THREAD	TENSION
Left needle	polyester cotton thread	balanced
Upper looper	metallic thread or floss	balanced
Lower looper	metallic thread or floss	balanced

Stitch length: 1 – 2
Differential feed: Depends on the thickness of the fabric
• The moving blade must be in the cutting position.

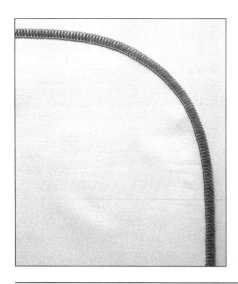

THREE-THREAD WIDE OVERLOCKING WITH EMBROIDERY THREAD

1. Place WS of fabric together and sew, using three-thread wide overlocking.

NEEDLE	THREAD	TENSION
Left needle	polyester cotton thread	balanced
Upper looper	embroidery thread	0 – 1 (loosen)
Lower looper	polyester cotton thread	balanced

Stitch length: 2 – 3
Differential feed: Depends on the thickness of the fabric
• The moving blade must be in the cutting position.

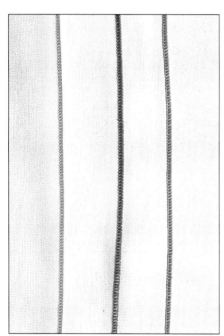

NARROW HEM WITH POLYESTER COTTON THREAD OR FLOSS

> **NOTE: The looper stitches must lock at the edge of the fabric.**

1. To sew a narrow hem, change to rolled hem plate or attachment.

2. Always sew on a single layer of fabric.

3. Pull the fabric gently at the back while sewing to ensure even stitching.

NEEDLE	THREAD	TENSION
Right needle	polyester cotton thread	balanced
Upper looper	polyester cotton thread or floss	balanced
Lower looper	polyester cotton thread or floss	balanced

Stitch length: 1 – 1½ /R
Differential feed: Depends on the thickness of the fabric
• The moving blade must be in the cutting position.

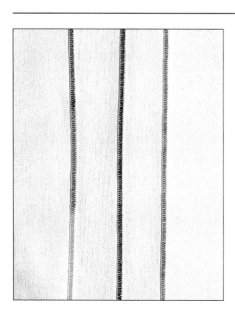

NARROW HEM WITH METALLIC THREAD

1. To sew a narrow hem, change to rolled hem plate or attachment.

2. Always sew on a single layer of fabric and ensure that the looper stitches lock at the edge of the fabric.

3. Pull the fabric gently at the back while sewing to ensure that the stitching is even.

NEEDLE	THREAD	TENSION
Right needle	polyester cotton thread	balanced
Upper looper	metallic thread	balanced
Lower looper	metallic thread	balanced

Stitch length: 1 – 1½ /R
Differential feed: Depends on the thickness of the fabric
• The moving blade must be in the cutting position.

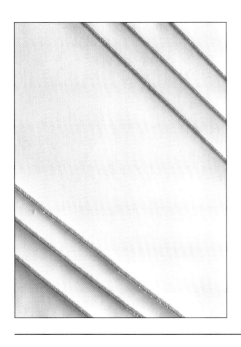

PIN-TUCKS WITH NARROW HEM

> NOTE: The looper stitches must lock at the edge of the fabric.

1. To sew pin-tucks, change to rolled hem plate or attachment.

2. Fold the fabric double and keep the fold in line with the edge of the plate while sewing.

NEEDLE	THREAD	TENSION
Right needle	polyester cotton thread	balanced
Upper looper	polyester cotton thread	
	or metallic thread	balanced
Lower looper	polyester cotton thread	
	or metallic thread	balanced

Stitch length: 1 – 1½ /R
Differential feed: Depends on the thickness of the fabric
• The moving blade must be disengaged.

LATTICE-WORK WITH DISSOLVING PLASTIC AND NARROW HEM

1. To do lattice-work, change to rolled hem plate or attachment.

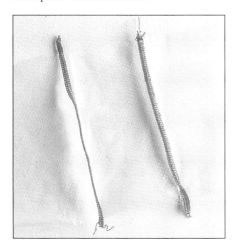

2. Feed the embroidery thread through under the foot.

3. Fold the dissolving plastic double and sew, keeping the embroidery thread on top.

4. Once the stitching has been completed and sewn onto the fabric on all sides, hold the fabric under cold running water. As the plastic has a gelatine base, it will dissolve and only the stitching will remain. Leave the article to dry.

NEEDLE	THREAD	TENSION
Right needle	Polyester cotton thread	balanced
Upper looper	Polyester cotton thread	
	or metallic thread	balanced
Lower looper	Polyester cotton thread	
	or metallic thread	balanced

Stitch length: 1 – 1½ /R
Differential feed: 1.0
• The moving blade can be in the cutting position or disengaged.

PLAITED CORD

Make your own braid by sewing over nylon cord or elastic, using decorative thread in different colours in the loopers. Feed the cord or elastic through under the pressure foot and sew, using three-thread overlocking. Plait the cord or braid to form a string.

NEEDLE	THREAD	TENSION
Right needle	polyester cotton thread	balanced
Upper looper	decorative thread	balanced
Lower looper	decorative thread	balanced

Stitch length: 1 – 2
Differential feed: 1.0
• The moving blade must be disengaged.

GATHERING WITH DIFFERENTIAL FEED

This method of gathering is suitable for light-weight fabrics and lace and can only be used on overlockers fitted with a differential feed.

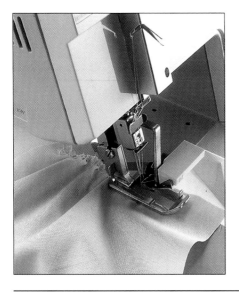

NOTE: Should you prefer more gathers, tighten the needle tension to 7 - 8.

1. Place the fabric or lace to be gathered at the bottom and the fabric onto which it must be gathered, on top.

2. With RS together, start by sewing a few stitches. Continue sewing slowly, while keeping the top fabric back slightly and feeding the bottom fabric or lace through under the pressure foot. Depending on the type of fabric or lace used and the extent to which the top fabric is kept back, the bottom fabric will be gathered.

NEEDLE	THREAD	TENSION
Left needle	polyester cotton thread	balanced
Right needle	polyester cotton thread	balanced
Upper looper	polyester cotton thread or floss	balanced
Lower looper	polyester cotton thread or floss	balanced

Stitch length: 4
Differential feed: 1.5 for very fine fabric and nylon lace
2.0 for light-weight fabrics and broderie anglaise
• The moving blade must be in the cutting position.

GATHERING OVER EMBROIDERY THREAD

This method is suitable for gathering one layer of fabric or lace, for example a frill for a cushion.

1. Measure the circumference of the article to be gathered and allow an extra 5 – 7 cm (2 – 2¾ in) of embroidery thread for tying a knot at the back and for thread to hold onto in front.

2. Feed the embroidery thread through under the pressure foot.

3. Pull on the embroidery thread while sewing so as to gather the fabric or lace at the back. When the sewing has been completed, the fabric will be gathered and the frill, for example, can then be pinned to the article.

NOTE: A special elastic or cording foot, through which the embroidery thread can be fed, is available for some makes and models of overlocker.

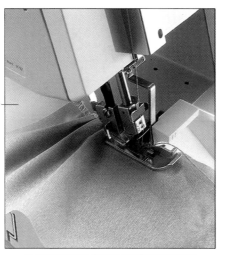

GATHERING OVER EMBROIDERY THREAD

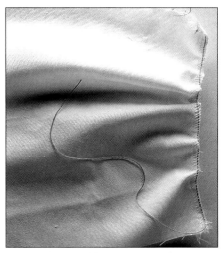

THE GATHERED FABRIC

NEEDLE	THREAD	TENSION
Right needle	polyester cotton thread	balanced
Upper looper	polyester cotton thread or floss	balanced
Lower looper	polyester cotton thread or floss	balanced

Stitch length: 3 – 4
Differential feed: 1.0
• The moving blade must be in the cutting position.

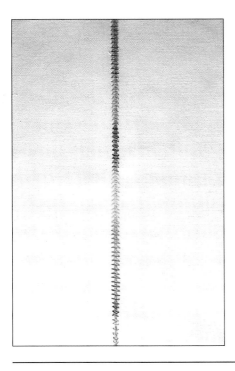

FAGGOTING WITH METALLIC THREAD

1. To join two pieces of fabric together, fold the seam allowance towards the wrong side of the fabric and press.

2. Place the folded edges with RS together. Place the folded edges under the pressure foot and sew as close as possible to the edge, using a seam or cloth guide to sew straight. Loose loops will form on the edge of the fabric.

3. Pull the seam open and press.

Optional: Place fabric in a contrasting colour behind the opening to enhance the faggoting.

NEEDLE	THREAD	TENSION
Left needle	metallic thread	0 – 1 (loosen)
Upper looper	polyester cotton thread	0 – 1 (loosen)
Lower looper	polyester cotton thread	5 – 8 (tighten)
	or floss	2 – 5 (tighten)

Stitch length: 2 – 3
Differential feed: Depends on the thickness of the fabric
• The moving blade must be disengaged.

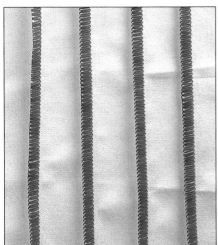

THREE-THREAD WIDE PIN-TUCKS

Either the left or the right needle can be used, depending on the desired width of the pin-tuck.

1. Place the WS of the fabric together and sew, using three-thread overlocking.

2. Press seam.

NEEDLE	THREAD	TENSION
Left needle	polyester cotton thread	balanced
Upper looper	metallic thread or floss	balanced
Lower looper	metallic thread or floss	balanced

Stitch length: 1 – 2
Differential feed: Depends on the thickness of the fabric
• The moving blade can be in the cutting position or disengaged.

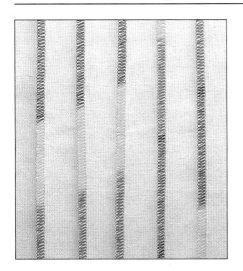

THREE-THREAD PIN-TUCKS

1. Using a marking pen, mark the lines for the pin-tucks on the fabric.

2. Fold the fabric in half, WS together, and sew as many pin-tucks as desired, keeping the fold of the fabric in line with the edge of the plate.

NEEDLE	THREAD	TENSION
Right needle	polyester cotton thread	balanced
Upper looper	metallic thread or floss	balanced
Lower looper	metallic thread or floss	balanced

Stitch length: 1 – 2
Differential feed: 1.0
• The moving blade must be disengaged.

TWISTED PIN-TUCKS WITH CHAIN STITCH

This technique can only be used on a five-thread overlocker.

1. Mark five parallel lines lengthwise 4 – 5 cm (1½ – 2 in) apart and centred on the fabric. Fold the fabric and press along each line.

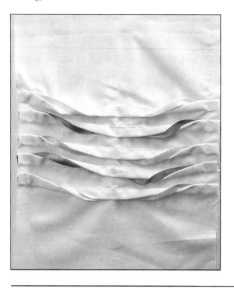

2. Mark five parallel lines widthwise at equal distances apart over whole width of fabric.

3. Keeping fold of fabric in line with the edge of the plate and using chain stitch, sew 7 – 9 mm-wide (¼ in-wide) pin-tucks lengthwise on the marked lines.

4. Place the left edge of the ribbon under each tuck at the top of the square. Keeping the ribbon right side up, carry it over the fold of the tuck and place the right edge of the ribbon next to the stitching line at the marked line. Fold the tuck over the ribbon. Pin.

5. Keeping the ribbon right side up, carry it from the marked line and over the tuck, placing the left edge of the ribbon next to the stitching line at the centre fold. Fold the tuck over the ribbon. Pin.

6. Continue with tuck.

7. Repeat for each ribbon.

8. Using the sewing machine and straight stitch, sew ribbon tucks in the direction of the folded tuck. Sew straight stitch only on the area covered with tucks.

NEEDLE	THREAD	TENSION
Chain needle	polyester cotton thread	balanced
Chain looper	polyester cotton thread	balanced

Stitch length: 2 – 3½
Differential feed: 1.0
• The moving blade must be disengaged.

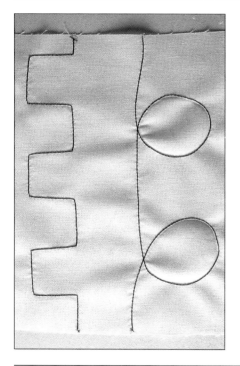

CHAIN STITCH WITH METALLIC THREAD

This technique can only be used on a five-thread overlocker.

NOTE: On some makes of over-locker, a special sewing table can be attached which enables you to sew a straight stitch in the centre of the fabric. This is used mainly for decorative stitching. Sew on a single layer of fabric, with the wrong side facing. Sew circles, corners and squares on the front of the article.

NEEDLE	THREAD	TENSION
Chain needle	polyester cotton thread	balanced
Chain looper	metallic thread	loosen tension

Stitch length: 3 – 4
Differential feed: 1.0
• The moving blade must be disengaged.

PRODUCTS USED FOR PROJECTS

FUSIBLE WEBBING
Fusible webbing is used inside a hem to attach it to the article. Press the hem firmly with a hot, dry iron – hold for ten seconds, then allow the fabric to cool for ten minutes. The webbing will disappear and the hem will adhere to the garment. Fusible webbing is available from specialist needlework shops and haberdashers.

DRESSMAKERS' TRACING PAPER
Several types exist for tracing patterns, and as a tear-off backing for embroidery, appliqué and cut-work. These are available from specialist needlework shops and haberdashers.

MARKING PEN

Purple and blue water-soluble pens are used for marking lines to act as guides when sewing. The purple marking pen will fade after a while, depending on the kind of fabric used. The blue marking pen on the other hand, will disappear when held under cold running water or when rubbed with a cold, damp cloth. Both marking pens are available from haberdashers.

FABRIC CRAYONS AND PENS

These are fully washable and fade-proof textile crayons to use on fabric. To fix the colours, iron the back of the fabric with a medium-hot iron once the ink is completely dry. Fabric crayons are available from stationery shops and haberdashers.

STITCH SEALANT

A transparent stitch or seam sealant such as Fray Check can be used to secure the ends of threads. It leaves no marks and when ironed, does not melt. Once completely dry, it remains soft and can therefore be used on fabric for clothing. Apart from its use when sewing with an overlocker, it can also be used to stop a run in hosiery or to secure threads after sewing on buttons. Stitch sealant is available from specialist needlework shops and haberdashers.

A SELECTION OF PRODUCTS USED IN THE MAKING OF PROJECTS

DISSOLVING PLASTIC

Dissolving plastic is used with an overlocker or sewing machine to create a lattice effect on fabric. Once the stitching is complete, the fabric is held under cold running water. As the plastic has a gelatine base, it dissolves and only the stitching remains. The article should then be left to dry. Dissolving plastic is available from specialist needlework shops and haberdashers.

PVA ADHESIVE

Mixed with water (1:4), PVA adhesive can be used to stiffen bows and small fabric bags. The adhesive is either painted onto the fabric or the fabric is dipped into the adhesive, then squeezed out and left to dry. It is important to use PVA Adhesive indoors and at room temperature. PVA is available from art and craft shops.

WADDING

Available in either cotton or polyester, this is used for quilting, duvets and wall-hangings. Polyester wadding is available in various weights and is easier to handle and clean than cotton. Wadding is available from specialist needlework shops and haberdashers.

IRON-ON INTERFACING

Iron-on interfacing is available in different weights, depending on the fabric for which it will be used. It is fully washable and can also be dry-cleaned. It is available from specialist needlework shops and haberdashers.

PVC (Polyvinyl chloride)

A waterproof substance usually backed by plain or printed cotton. Lightweight types are easy to handle and more suitable for baby items.

PLACEMAT BATTING

When making placemats and pot holders, it is essential to use a special type of batting which is heat resistant and which will retain its shape when washed. Placemat batting is a thin, compressed batting which is available from specialist needlework shops and haberdashers.

ACRYLIC GLAZE

An acrylic glaze or varnish such as Modge Podge can be used as a sealant for fabric bows and small fabric bags. It also gives the completed article additional shine and prevents the stiffened article from losing its shape. It can also be used to protect fabric-covered pot-plant holders and tea-trays. Modge Podge is available from craft shops, while acrylic varnish can be purchased from DIY outlets.

THE ENTRANCE HALL

When decorating your home, it is important to have one main colour, or shades of that colour, represented in each room.

In this particular home, the colour blue, used in different shades and combinations, appears in each room. All the colours used in the interior of this home are introduced in the covered mirror in the entrance hall.

COVERED OVAL MIRROR
WITH FLATLOCK DECORATION

The mirror featured in the photograph shows the tailored bow described in steps 16 – 20, but a simple bow in plain or printed fabric looks just as lovely.

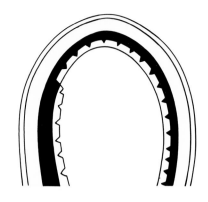

Fig. 1

REQUIREMENTS

65 cm x 55 cm (25½ in x 21½ in) white or plain fabric for front

Two 55 cm x 50 cm (21½ in x 19½ in) pieces of white or plain fabric for frame and backing

3 m x 9 cm-wide (3¼ yd x 3½ in-wide) plain or printed fabric for outer frill (2½ times the circumference of the outer edge of the mirror)

2 m x 14 cm-wide (2¼ yd x 5½ in-wide) plain or printed fabric for standard bow

OR

1.2 m x 25 cm-wide (1⅜ yd x 10 in-wide) plain fabric for first tailored bow

40 cm x 32 cm-wide (15¾ in x 12½ in-wide) plain fabric for second tailored bow

12 cm x 10 cm (4¾ in x 4 in) plain fabric for bow band

4 m x 5 cm-wide (4¼ yds x 2 in-wide) broderie anglaise for inner frill (3 times the circumference of the outer edge of the mirror)

1 m x 3 cm-wide (30 in x 1¼ in-wide) broderie anglaise for inner edge frill (optional)

2.6 m (2¾ yd) piping in matching colour for inner and outer edge of frame

Two 50 cm x 40 cm x 3 mm-thick (19½ in x 15¾ in x ⅛ in-thick) pieces hardboard or thin wood for frame and backing (frame is 7 cm [2¾ in] wide)

2 cm-thick (¾ in-thick) foam rubber cut 5 mm (¼ in) larger than frame's inner and outer edges

Embroidery thread

Metallic thread or floss in different colours

Polyester cotton thread to match fabric

Marking pen

Stitch sealant (see page 19)

Glue gun and glue sticks

Clear glue

Mirror tape

30 cm (12 in) long metal chain

Two small hooks

Six short screws

METHOD

1. Using marking pen, mark diagonal lines 4 cm (1½ in) apart on fabric measuring 65 cm x 55 cm (25½ in x 21½ in).

2. With WS together, sew **flatlocking with metallic thread** (see page 11) on marked lines, using different colours and working from the top of the mirror. Sew in one direction to ensure that all stitching is facing downwards in the same direction. Pull the seams open so that they lie flat, then press the fabric on the wrong side.

3. Glue pre-cut foam rubber to the wooden frame or to the rough side of the hardboard, using clear glue, and allow to dry.

4. Pull fabric measuring 55 cm x 45 cm (21½ in x 17¾ in) tightly over the foam rubber and frame and glue fabric to wooden frame or to smooth side of hardboard, using clear glue. Cut away any excess fabric.

5. Remove fabric from centre of frame by cutting fabric away 3 cm (1¼ in) from the inside edge. Clip fabric every 2 cm (¾ in), pull fabric taut and glue to back of frame (see Fig. 1).

6. Repeat with fabric decorated with flatlocking, ensuring that the flatlocking is straight.

7. Using clear glue, glue piping to the inner and outer edges of the mirror, overlapping ends at centre lower edge.

8. **Gather** lace for frill **over embroidery thread** (see page 16).

9. Using clear glue or glue gun, glue the broderie anglaise frill to the back of the outer edge of frame, starting at the centre lower edge of the mirror, overlapping ends.

10. If necessary, join strips of fabric for frill using three-thread overlocking to obtain the required length.

11. Edge the frill using **narrow hem with metallic thread or floss** (see page 14).

12. **Gather** frill **over embroidery thread** (see page 16).

13. Using clear glue or glue gun, glue frill to the back of the outer edge starting at the centre lower edge of the mirror, overlapping ends.

14. Should you prefer it, use clear glue or glue gun to glue the 1 m x 3 cm-wide (39 in x 1¼ in-wide) broderie anglaise to the inner edge of the mirror on top of the piping.

15. Cover the rough side of the hardboard backing with the 55 cm x 50 cm (22 in x 19½ in) fabric, pulling it tightly and glueing it to the smooth side.

16. *To make a tailored bow,* shape the short edges of the fabric. With RS together, fold fabric in half lengthwise and sew all round, using three- or four-thread overlocking. Undo 7 cm (2¾ in) of the overlocking in the centre of the long side by cutting and pulling on the

needle thread. Turn right side out. Close by hand using slipstitch or straight stitch on a sewing machine.

17. Fold the fabric in half widthwise and, using sewing machine and a straight stitch, sew 28 cm (11 in) from the fold. Open out fabric with seam at centre back (see Fig. 2).

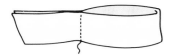

Fig. 2

18. With RS together, sew fabric strip for second bow all round, using three- or four-thread overlocking. Undo 5 – 7 cm (2 – 2¾ in) of the overlocking in the centre by cutting and pulling on the needle thread. Turn the fabric right side out and close by hand using slipstitch or using straight stitch on the sewing machine.

19. With RS together, sew bow band along long edge, using three- or four-thread overlocking. Turn the bow band right side out and position seam at centre back. Press.

20. Place second bow on top of first bow and pull bow band tightly around both bows (see Fig. 3). Secure at the back by hand (see Fig. 4).

Fig. 3

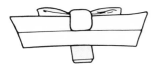

Fig. 4

21. *To make a standard bow*, shape short edges of fabric (see Fig. 5).

Fig. 5

THE OVAL MIRROR AND TELEPHONE BOOK COVER

22. Finish the edges all round in a contrasting colour using **narrow hem with metallic thread or floss** (see page 15). Secure ends with stitch sealant (see page 19).

23. Knot the fabric in the centre, then tie the ends into a bow as shown (see Fig. 6).

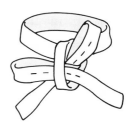

Fig. 6

24. Pull both loops tightly, ensuring that they are the same size (see Fig. 7).

Fig. 7

25. Glue bow to lower edge of centre front using the glue gun.

26. Stick mirror to hardboard or wood with mirror tape. Drill holes to join front and back sections of the frame and hang chain (see Fig. 8).

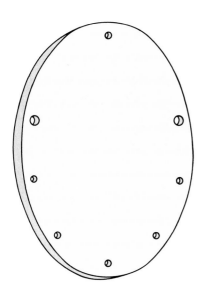

Fig. 8

COVERED TELEPHONE BOOK

The instructions given below are for a telephone book measuring about 52 cm x 31 cm (20½ in x 12¼ in), including a 1 cm (½ in) seam allowance. To make your own pattern, measure the length of the telephone book and add a 2 cm (¾ in) seam allowance plus 1 cm (½ in) for ease. Measure the width of the closed book and add a 2 cm (¾ in) seam allowance (see Fig. 9). Draw the pattern pieces on dressmakers' tracing paper before cutting out on the fabric.

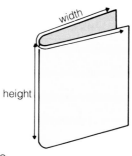

Fig. 9

REQUIREMENTS
Three 30 cm x 6 cm (12 in x 2¼ in) strips of fabric in three different colours (three printed and six plain in colours represented in the print) for patchwork insert
42 cm x 31 cm (16½ in x 12¼ in) plain fabric for front
Two 17 cm x 31 cm (6¾ in x 12¼ in) pieces of plain or printed fabric for inside flaps
42 cm x 31 cm (16½ in x 12¼ in) plain fabric for lining
3.4 m x 4 cm-wide (3¾ yd x 1½ in-wide) broderie anglaise for outer edge
52 cm x 31 cm (20½ in x 12¼ in) thin wadding
Two 17 cm x 31 cm (6¾ in x 12¼ in) pieces of iron-on interlining for inside flaps
Dressmakers' tracing paper
Embroidery thread
Polyester cotton thread to match fabric
Stitch sealant (see page 19)
Marking pen

METHOD

1. Cut a rectangular window measuring 31 cm x 12 cm (12¼ in x 4¾ in) in the tracing paper.

2. With WS together, join strips for patchwork insert using **flatlocking with embroidery thread** (see page 12). Pull open and press. Place window in tracing paper on the joined patchwork fabric and turn window to a 45 degree angle so that the stripes run diagonally (see Fig. 10). Cut out the rectangle of fabric.

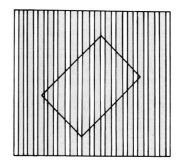

Fig. 10

3. Mark the centre of front cover with a marking pen and cut along marked line. With WS together and keeping insert on top, join the patchwork insert to front cover, using **flatlocking with embroidery thread** (see page 12).

4. Pin wadding to WS of cover.

5. **Gather** the broderie anglaise for the frill **over embroidery thread** (see page 16).

6. With RS together, pin the frill to the outer edge of the cover and sew all round, using a three-thread overlocking, starting anew at each corner and overlapping the ends.

7. Iron the interlining onto fabric for flaps. Finish one long edge of each flap using three-thread overlocking.

8. Finish short edges of lining using three-thread overlocking.

9. With RS together, place flaps on short edges of cover, and then place lining on top, WS up (see Fig. 11).

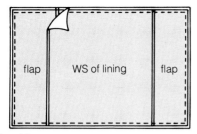

Fig. 11

10. Sew round all four edges using three-, four- or five-thread overlocking, starting anew at every corner.

11. Knot loose threads at each corner and work away by hand or secure the ends with stitch sealant. Turn the cover right side out.

WELCOME WINDOW HOOPS

REQUIREMENTS
Lightweight fabric (for example, net or organza), cut 3 cm (1¼ in) larger than the diameter of the ring
5 – 7 cm-wide (2 – 2¾ in-wide) broderie anglaise, measuring twice the circumference of the embroidery ring
1 m x 7 mm – 1 cm-wide (1⅛ yd x ¼ –½ in-wide) ribbon
Insert lace or broderie anglaise for decoration on inside (optional)
Embroidery thread
Metallic thread or floss
Polyester cotton thread to match fabric
40, 50 or 60 cm-diameter (8, 10 or 12 in-diameter) wooden embroidery ring
Clear glue

METHOD
1. Decorate the lightweight fabric with lace and **flatlocking with metallic thread or floss** (see page 12).

2. Place fabric over inner ring, place outer ring over inner ring and tighten screw to pull fabric taut. Trim the excess at the back to 1 cm (½ in).

AN ATTRACTIVE WELCOME WINDOW HOOP

3. Glue fabric to back of outer ring.

4. **Gather** broderie anglaise **over embroidery thread** (see page 16).

5. Apply glue to the outer ring and allow glue to dry slightly before positioning the lace. Start from the screw on the embroidery ring and work around, pressing the lace on firmly and overlapping the ends.

6. Decorate with a ribbon tied into a bow around screw. Attach a length of

ribbon to back and hang on inside of front or entrance hall window.

HINT
These hoops can be used to decorate your front door at Christmas. Use Christmas fabric instead of broderie anglaise for the frill around the outer edge of the embroidery ring. Finish edge of frill using **narrow hem with metallic thread** (see page 15).

THE LOUNGE

For the lounge, a combination of warm pink and navy has been used. To add interest and to soften the severity of the plain colours, a porcelain pink floral fabric has been used for the frilled overlay, in the tie-backs and as binding on the draped curtains.

CURTAINS

Curtains form a very important part of the decor and should therefore be chosen very carefully. They create atmosphere, add warmth and improve the general appearance of a room, and can also be used to camouflage problem areas and create optical illusions.

CURTAIN FABRIC

Before calculating the amount of fabric needed, decide on the type of curtain you wish to make, the desired length of the curtain and the type of heading tape you wish to use. Should you decide on fabric with a definite pattern, this will have to be taken into consideration when buying the fabric. The width of the fabric, too, will also affect the amount you buy. Buy good quality fabric that will not fade, lose its colour or shrink during washing.

CURTAIN RODS AND TRACKS

It is important to fit curtain tracks or rods before you take the measurements for the curtains. The shape and size of the window as well as the style of the curtains will influence your decision to use curtain tracks, rods with rings or spring wire.

CURTAIN HEADINGS

Cotton or nylon gathering tape is suitable for lightweight, sheer or net curtains and for valances, while Kirsch tape for pencil or pinch pleats is more suitable for heavyweight linen or cotton curtains. Tape has cords which are pulled up to form pleats and gathers, or slots into which curtain hooks or pronged hooks are inserted.

Sheer or net curtains are usually fitted inside the window recess, using spring wire, tracks or rods with rings. Heavyweight curtains are hung from a track or rod which extends past the window to let in the maximum amount of light when the curtains are open.

CALCULATING THE AMOUNT OF FABRIC REQUIRED

To calculate the width of *sheer and net curtains*, measure the width of the curtain track or the window recess and multiply by 2½ – 3, for necessary full-

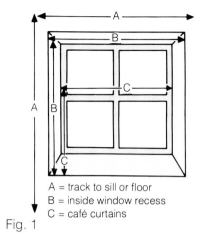

A = track to sill or floor
B = inside window recess
C = café curtains

Fig. 1

ness if using spring wire or gathering tape. To calculate the length, measure the length of the window recess from the spring wire or track to the window sill and add on 15 – 20 cm (6 – 8 in) for seam and hem allowances (see Fig. 1).

To calculate the width of a *gathered curtain* or *curtain with pencil pleats* for light- or heavy-weight curtains, measure the length of the track or rod and multiply by 2½ – 3 to obtain the necessary fullness.

To calculate the width of a curtain with *pinch pleats*, measure the length of the track or rod and multiply by 2¼ – 2½ (see Fig. 1).

It may sometimes be necessary to join the fabric to obtain the desired width. Divide the fabric width into the measured width of the curtain to calculate the number of drops required.

To calculate the length of the curtain, measure the distance from the track or rod to the desired length of the curtain and add on 20 cm (8 in) for hem and seam allowances (see Fig. 1).

To calculate the total amount of fabric required, multiply the length of the drop (including the hem and seam allowance) by the number of drops needed. Buy too much rather than too little fabric, so as to ensure that the curtains have the necessary fullness.

VALANCES

Should you wish to cover the pelmets, a gathered valance can be used irrespective of the style of the curtain. A valance can be mounted or nailed onto a wooden pelmet with upholstery tacks, or hung in front of a double track.

CALCULATING THE AMOUNT OF FABRIC REQUIRED

A valance is fully gathered across the width and length and is usually one sixth of the length of the curtain, but never shorter than 20 cm (8 in). Use the same colour fabric, contrasting or printed fabric for the valance. The edge of the valance can be finished off with a frill in a contrasting colour or broderie anglaise. Gathering tape can be sewn onto the valance and pulled up to make a mock festoon valance.

To calculate the width, measure the length of the track, rod or pelmet and multiply by 2½ – 3. Calculate the amount of heading or gathering tape required in the same way. To calculate the length, measure one sixth of the curtain length.

If you are making a mock festoon valance, measure ⅙ of the curtain length, multiply by 3 and add on 10 cm (4 in) for seam and hem allowances.

DRAPED CURTAINS

Draped curtains are ideal for creating a more informal look and can be used on their own or in conjunction with conventional curtains. Drapes in two or more colours can be used together and they may be edged with lace or bias binding in a contrasting colour. The fabric can be draped over swagholders to create interesting effects. This eliminates the expense of fitting an additional track or rod. Swagholders are obtainable in white and brass and are easily fitted. Swagholders are also used to create rosettes (see Fig. 2).

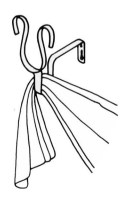

Fig. 2

WARM PINK CURTAINS WITH PINCH PLEATS HELD BACK WITH PLAITED TIE-BACKS

CALCULATING THE AMOUNT OF FABRIC REQUIRED

To calculate the amount of fabric required for draped curtains, measure the distance between the swagholders, and from the top of the window to the required length, and multiply by 2.

LINING

It is always advisable to line curtains as sunlight weakens the fibres. Made from pure cotton, a lining can be sewn separately or together with the curtain onto heading or gathering tape.

CALCULATING THE AMOUNT OF FABRIC REQUIRED

To calculate the amount of fabric needed for the lining, follow the instructions given above for curtains.

TIE-BACKS

Tie-backs not only add a professional finish to curtains, but also serve a practical purpose in that they hold back the curtains and allow the maximum amount of daylight into the room.

The length of the tie-back will depend on the number of drops used to make up the curtains and the type of fabric used: heavier curtains, for example, will require longer tie-backs. The shape and size of the tie-back will also depend on the style of the curtain. Tie-backs may be plain, plaited, edged with piping, frills, fringes or pleats and decorated with bows or rosettes.

Although tie-backs are usually positioned two-thirds of the way down the length of the curtain, other factors may influence their position.

Use a tape measure to hold back the curtain to determine the correct length of the tie-back.

CURTAINS WITH PINCH PLEATS

REQUIREMENTS
Fabric as measured (see page 28)
Heading tape for pinch pleats,
    equal to the width of the curtain
    as measured, plus 10 cm (4 in)
    to fold under on either side
Polyester cotton thread to
    match fabric
Stitch sealant (see page 19)
Pronged hooks

METHOD
1. If necessary, join fabric lengthwise using three-, four-, or five-thread overlocking to obtain the correct width for the necessary fullness.

2. Finish all the edges using three-thread overlocking.

3. Fold long edges back 2 cm (¾ in) and, using sewing machine, sew with a straight stitch.

4. Fold bottom edge back 5 cm (2 in) and either sew with **blind hem foot** (see page 8) or turn bottom edge back 5 cm (2 in) and, using the sewing machine, sew with a straight stitch.

5. Fold the top edge of each curtain back 10 cm (4 in) and press.

6. Position heading tape 3 cm (1¼ in) from top edge and pin. Fold raw edges of tape back 5 cm (2 in) on either side and, using sewing machine, sew with straight stitch.

7. Insert pronged hooks and hang up the curtains (see Fig. 3).

Fig. 3

DRAPED CURTAINS

REQUIREMENTS
Fabric as measured (see page 28)
4 cm-wide (1½ in-wide) pre-cut
    bias binding in contrasting
    colour, measuring twice the
    width and once the length of
    the fabric for draped curtains
Polyester cotton thread to
    match fabric

METHOD
1. Insert bias binding into **bias binder** (see page 9) and sew along two short edges and one long edge of the curtain fabric, using chain stitch.

2. Sew remaining long edge using three-thread overlocking.

3. Drape fabric onto swagholders.

PLAITED TIE-BACKS

Neither the colours nor the fabric need be the same as the curtains but a combination of two plain and one printed fabric is very successful.

REQUIREMENTS
For each tie-back:
Three 13 cm-wide (5¼ in-wide)
    pieces of fabric the length of
    the tie-back as measured
    (approximately 50 – 100 cm
    [19½ – 39½ in])
Polyester cotton thread to
    match fabric
Polyester filling
Two plastic rings

METHOD
1. With RS together, fold each piece of fabric lengthwise and sew long edge using three-thread overlocking. Turn tubes right side out and position seams at centre back. Press.

2. Join one short side of the three tubes together using three-thread overlocking. Fold back 1 cm (½ in) and slipstitch by hand (see Fig. 4a).

Fig. 4a   Fig. 4b

3. Fill tubes with polyester filling.

4. Plait tubes and secure ends with slipstitch (see Fig. 4b).

5. Attach a plastic ring to each end of the tie-back.

CUSHIONS WITH PIPING

The instructions given below are for cushions measuring 38 cm x 38 cm (15 in x 15 in), including a 1 cm (½ in) seam allowance.

SQUARE CUSHION

REQUIREMENTS
45 cm x 45 cm (17¾ in x 17¾ in)
    plain fabric for front
Two 40 cm x 25 cm (15¾ in x
    10 in) pieces of fabric for back
40 cm x 40 cm (15¾ in x 15¾ in)
    calico for inner cushion
1.7 m x 4 cm-wide (1⅞ yd x
    1½ in) pre-made bias binding
    in contrasting colour (see
    page 10)
1.7 m (1⅞ yd) nylon cord for
    piping
Embroidery thread
Metallic thread
Polyester cotton thread or floss to
    match fabric
Polyester filling
Marking pen
Stitch sealant (see page 19)

METHOD

1. Decorate the fabric for the front of the cushion using **flatlocking with embroidery thread** (see page 12) or **pin-tucks with narrow hem** (see page 15), then press.

2. Cut fabric to measure 40 cm x 40 cm (15¾ in x 15¾ in).

3. To make piping, insert the nylon cord into the bias binding and sew on RS as close as possible to the cord, using the sewing machine and zipper foot.

4. Using sewing machine and zipper foot, sew piping onto the cushion front 1 cm (½ in) from the edge. At the corners, clip piping 1.5 cm (½ in) from the edge, and turn to make a square corner (see Fig. 5).

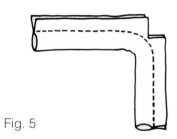

Fig. 5

5. When you reach the starting point, unpick approximately 3 cm (1¼ in) of the stitching. Trim the cord, ensuring that you do not cut it too short or leave it too long as this will cause a ridge.

6. Fold the bias fabric back 1 cm (½ in) and position it over the piping at the starting point and stitch in place (see Fig. 6).

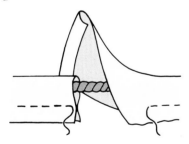

Fig. 6

7. Finish one long edge of each piece of fabric for cushion back using three-thread overlocking. Fold back 1 cm (½ in) and, using sewing machine, sew with straight stitch.

8. With RS together, pin back panels to front. Using sewing machine and zipper foot, sew all round.

9. Finish edges using three-thread overlocking, starting anew at each corner (see Fig. 7). Secure the ends of the threads with stitch sealant.

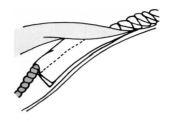

Fig. 7

10. With RS together, sew around edge of calico for inner cushion using three-thread overlocking. Undo 5 – 7 cm (2 – 2¾ in) and turn cover right side out.

11. Fill with polyester filling and close opening by hand using slipstitch.

ROUND CUSHION

REQUIREMENTS
45 cm x 45 cm (17¾ in x 17¾ in) plain fabric for front
Two 45 cm x 25 cm (17¾ in x 10 in) pieces of fabric for back
40 cm x 40 cm (15¾ in x 15¾ in) calico for inner cushion
1.7 m x 4 cm-wide (1⅞ yd x 1½ in) pre-made bias binding in a contrasting colour (see page 10)
1.7 m (1⅞ yd) nylon cord for piping
Embroidery thread
Metallic thread
Polyester cotton thread or floss to match fabric
Polyester filling
Marking pen
Stitch sealant (see page 19)

METHOD

1. Decorate cushion front using **flatlocking with embroidery thread** (see page 12) or **pin-tucks with narrow hem** (see page 15). Press.

2. Fold fabric for cushion front lengthwise, then crosswise to find the centre. Draw a quarter circle measuring 20 cm (8 in) from the centre. Cut out the circle of fabric.

3. Finish one long side of each piece of fabric for cushion back using three-thread overlocking. Turn edge back 1 cm (½ in) and, using sewing machine, sew with straight stitch.

4. Overlap hemmed edges by 4 cm (1½ in) and pin. Now fold fabric in half and in half again and trim to 20 cm (8 in) from centre.

5. Using the **tape guide and piping foot** (see page 9) and with RS together, sew piping between front and back of cushion using three- or four-thread overlocking, and overlap piping at the end (see Fig. 8).

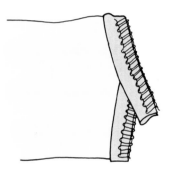

Fig. 8

NOTE: If you cannot fit a tape guide onto your overlocker, sew the piping using the sewing machine and the zipper foot and proceed as for square cushion.

6. Fold calico for inner cushion in half and then in half again. Draw a quarter circle measuring 20 cm (8 in).

7. With RS together, sew around edge of calico for inner cushion using three-thread overlocking. Undo 5 – 7 cm (2 – 2¾ in) by cutting and pulling on the needle thread, and turn cushion cover right side out.

8. Fill with polyester filling and close opening by hand using slipstitch.

ROUND TABLE-CLOTH

A round table covered with a full-length cloth and overlay forms a lovely focal point in any room, especially with a collection of ornaments or books or a single lamp on it. If you do not have a proper round table, use a circle of chipboard with a wooden or chipboard support. Even bricks can be used to support the table!

CALCULATING THE AMOUNT OF FABRIC REQUIRED

Measure from the centre of the table to the floor, and add a hem allowance of 1 cm (½ in) and multiply by 2 (see Fig. 9). This measurement represents the diameter of the table-cloth. If you are adding a frill, remember to subtract the width of the frill from this measurement on both sides.

If the diameter of your table-cloth is wider than the fabric width, the fabric will need to be joined to obtain the correct width. Join a strip of fabric along one or both sides of the centre piece to avoid a seam running down the centre of the cloth.

REQUIREMENTS
Fabric as measured
Metallic thread or floss
Polyester cotton thread to
  match fabric
Stitch sealant (see page 19)

METHOD

1. Fold fabric in half lengthwise and crosswise and cut a quarter circle the required size (see Fig. 10).

2. If necessary, join seam/seams at the side/sides using three-, four- or five-thread overlocking.

3. Finish the edge using **narrow hem with metallic thread or floss** (see page 15).

4. Seal ends with stitch sealant.

OVERLAY WITH FRILL

An overlay is very effective if made in a contrasting colour, especially when used with a full-length table-cloth.

Overlays can be round or square and be edged with a hem, a frill or a frill and piping. The instructions given below are for an overlay measuring 1 m x 1 m (1⅛ yd in x 1⅛ yd) including a 1 cm (½ in) seam allowance.

REQUIREMENTS
90 cm x 90 cm (35½ in x 35½ in)
  printed fabric
7.2 m x 12 cm-wide (8 yd x
  4¾ in-wide) printed fabric for
  frill (twice the circumference of
  the overlay)
3.7 m x 4 cm-wide (4 yd x
  1½ in-wide) pre-made bias
  binding in contrasting colour
  (see page 10)
3.7 m (4 yd) nylon cord for
  piping (the circumference
  of the overlay plus 10 cm
  [4 in] for ease)
Embroidery thread
Metallic thread or floss
Polyester cotton thread to
  match fabric
Stitch sealant (see page 19)

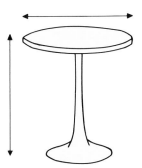

Fig. 9

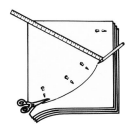

Fig. 10

A PLAIN ROUND TABLE-CLOTH IN WARM PINK FABRIC

A PINK FLORAL OVERLAY AND A TIFFANY LAMPSHADE

METHOD

1. With RS together, join short edges of fabric strips for frill to form a circle, using three-thread overlocking.

2. Finish long edge of frill using **narrow hem with metallic thread or floss** (see page 15).

3. To make the piping, insert the nylon cord into the bias binding and sew on the RS as close as possible to the cord, using the sewing machine and the zipper foot.

4. Using sewing machine and zipper foot, sew piping onto RS of overlay. At the corners, clip piping 1.5 cm (½ in) from the edge, and turn to make a square corner (see Fig. 11).

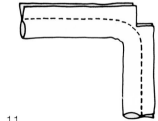

Fig. 11

5. **Gather** the frill **over embroidery thread** (see page 16).

6. With RS together, sew gathered frill to overlay using sewing machine and zipper foot, sewing as close as possible to the piping.

7. Finish edges all round with three-thread overlocking, starting anew at each corner.

8. Secure the ends of the threads with stitch sealant.

COVERED TIFFANY LAMPSHADE

CALCULATING THE AMOUNT OF FABRIC REQUIRED

Measure the height of the lampshade and add on an 8 cm (3¼ in) hem and seam allowance at the top and bottom. Measure the circumference of the lampshade and add on 3 cm (1¼ in) for the seam allowance.

REQUIREMENTS

Fabric for lampshade
   as measured
12 cm-wide (4¾ in-wide) printed
   fabric for frill, measuring
   2½ times the circumference of
   the lampshade
7 cm-wide (2¾ in-wide) white or
   plain fabric for second frill,
   measuring 2½ times the
   circumference of the
   lampshade
3 cm-wide (1¼ in-wide) broderie
   anglaise, measuring 2½ times
   the circumference of the
   lampshade, for second frill
1 m x 5 cm-wide (1⅛ yd x
   2 in-wide) printed fabric for
   lattice work
1.1 m x 2.5 cm-wide (1¼ yd x
   1 in-wide) ribbon for elastic
   casing
4/6 cord elastic for casings at the
   top and bottom and ribbon
   casing
Embroidery thread
Metallic thread or floss
Polyester cotton thread to
   match fabric
Marking pen
1 m x 8 cm-wide (1⅛ yd x
   3¼ in-wide) dissolving plastic
   (see page 19)
Stitch sealant (see page 19)
Metal frame for lampshade

METHOD

1. Using a marking pen, draw a line on fabric for the lampshade 4 cm (1½ in) from the top edge and another 6 – 8 cm (2¼ – 3¼ in) from the bottom edge. All decorative stitching must be sewn between these two lines.

2. From the top marked line, sew 2 – 3 rows **flatlocking with embroidery thread** (see page 12) 2 – 3cm (¾ – 1¼ in) apart. Pull open so that stitching lies flat. Press fabric on WS.

3. Cut printed fabric for lattice-work into 8 cm x 5 cm (3¼ in x 2 in) pieces according to the number of metal ribs on the frame.

4. Fold dissolving plastic in half and sew **lattice-work with dissolving plastic and narrow hem** (see page 15).

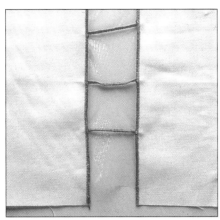

DISSOLVING PLASTIC

5. With WS together, sew dissolving plastic to fabric using **narrow hem with metallic thread** (see page 15), ensuring that the lattice-work will be positioned between the metal ribs of the lampshade.

6. Using a marking pen, draw a line 4 cm (1½ in) down from the flatlocking and cut along this line.

7. Join fabric with lattice-work to the rest of the lampshade at top and bottom using **narrow hem with metallic thread** (see page 15).

8. Lay the fabric flat and pour cold water over fabric and dissolving plastic, which will then disappear. Keep the fabric flat and allow to dry. Do not pull on fabric while it is still wet.

9. Using three-thread overlocking, sew fabric with RS together to form a circle, ensuring top and bottom edges and decorative stitchings are in line and that cover fits tightly over lampshade.

10. With RS together, sew the short edges of the fabric for the first frill, using three-thread overlocking.

11. Finish both long edges of first frill using **narrow hem with metallic thread** (see page 15).

12. Attach the broderie anglaise to the second frill with RS together, using **flatlocking with metallic thread** (see page 11). Sew the short edges to form a circle, using three-thread overlocking.

13. Finish top edge of second frill using **narrow hem with metallic thread** (page 15).

14. Gather both frills on sewing machine 1 cm (½ in) from the top edge using a wide zig-zag stitch and by threading the embroidery thread through underneath the sewing foot. Knot the embroidery thread at the back. While sewing, pull the embroidery thread in front so that fabric gathers at the back. (The length of the embroidery thread equals the circumference of the lampshade plus 10 cm [4 in] for ease.)

15. Using a sewing machine and straight stitch, sew frills 6 – 8 cm (2¼ – 3¼ in) from the bottom edge.

16. Finish the top and bottom edges of the lampshade cover, using three-thread overlocking.

17. Fold top edge back 1 cm (½ in) to form a casing and sew, using sewing machine and straight stitch, leaving a small opening.

18. Fold bottom edge back 2 cm (¾ in) to form a casing and sew, using sewing machine and straight stitch, leaving a small opening.

19. Use the sewing machine and straight stitch to sew ribbon for elastic casing on WS of fabric 6 cm (2¼ in) from top edge, overlapping the ends.

20. Pull the elastic through the top, bottom and ribbon casings and fit the lampshade over the metal frame. Pull the elastic tightly and knot.

THE KITCHEN

The combination of plain and floral fabrics in yellow and navy blue gives this kitchen a sunny look. Frilled cushions and tea cosy are successfully combined with stylish, piped appliance covers, a plain table-cloth and pot holder.

SCALLOPED CAFÉ CURTAIN

This café curtain is a fixed curtain attached with loops or rings to a rod or pole and is hung across the lower half of a window. The top edge of the curtain may be scalloped and have loops or pinch pleats.

CALCULATING THE AMOUNT OF FABRIC REQUIRED

For a scalloped top edge with loops, measure the length of the rod and multiply by 1½. For a scalloped top edge with pinch pleats, multiply the length of the rod by 2.

To calculate the length of the curtain, measure the distance from the rod (usually positioned in the lower half of the window) to the window sill.

Decide on the number and width of the loops and the width of the scallops in between them. Remember to allow for enough fabric to go over the rod, and to hang down at least 10 cm (4 in). Cut a paper template to measure for the loops and scallops.

A SCALLOPED CAFÉ CURTAIN PROVIDES PRIVACY WHILE LETTING IN SUNLIGHT

A facing or lining can be used to strengthen the loops. Cut the facing/lining the same width as the curtain and the length of the loops plus 10 cm (4 in).

REQUIREMENTS
Fabric for curtain as measured
Facing as measured (optional)
10 cm-wide (4 in-wide) printed fabric measuring the same as the width of the curtain
3 – 5 mm-wide (⅛ – ¼ in-wide) ribbon measuring twice the width of curtain
2 m x 3 – 5 mm-wide (2¼ yd x ⅛ – ¼ in-wide) ribbon in contrasting colour for bows
Metallic thread
Polyester cotton thread to match fabric
Paper template
Marking pen

METHOD

1. Position the template on the fabric and cut out the tabs and scallops.

2. With WS of facing and curtain fabric together, sew around the edges of the loops using **three-thread wide overlocking with metallic thread** (see page 13).

3. Finish top ends of loops using three-thread overlocking. Turn the loops back 10 – 12 cm (4 – 4¾ in) and finish off by hand.

4. Finish edge of facing using three-thread overlocking.

5. Mark lines for decoration on curtain as shown (see Fig. 1).

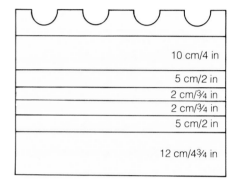

Fig. 1

6. Sew **flatlocking over ribbon with metallic thread or floss** (see page 12) on marked lines.

7. Sew **three-thread pin-tucks** (see page 17) on marked lines.

8. Pin the printed fabric to the lower edge of the curtain.

9. Keeping the printed fabric on top, sew the top edge of the fabric to the curtain using **flatlocking with metallic thread** (see page 11).

10. Sew lower edge of printed fabric to lower edge of curtain using **three-thread wide overlocking with metallic thread** (see page 13).

11. Finish sides of curtain using **three-thread wide overlocking with metallic thread** (see page 13).

12. Make bows and sew them on by hand 12 cm (4¾ in) apart in the centre of flatlocking over ribbon.

VALANCE

CALCULATING THE AMOUNT OF FABRIC REQUIRED

To calculate the amount of fabric required, refer to page 28.

REQUIREMENTS
Fabric as measured
Metallic thread
Polyester cotton thread to
    match fabric
Gathering tape
Curtain hooks (if using a
    double track)
Upholstery tacks (if mounting
    on a pelmet)

METHOD

1. Finish lower edge of valance using **narrow hem with metallic thread** (see page 15).

2. Fold short sides of valance back 2 cm (¾ in) and, using sewing machine, sew with straight stitch.

3. Fold top edge of valance back 10 cm (4 in) and press. Using sewing machine, sew heading tape 3 – 4 cm (1¼ – 1½ in) from the edge of the fabric.

4. Insert curtain hooks and hang or mount the valance on the pelmet, using upholstery tacks.

SEAT CUSHION AND COVER

To make a pattern for the seat cushion, place tracing paper or paper on the chair seat, trace the outline and then cut out the template, adding a 1 cm (½ in) seam allowance all round if you do not intend adding a frill.

If you intend adding a frill, measure the outer edge of the seat and multiply by 2½ – 3. Cut the fabric for the frill approximately 8 – 10 cm (3¼ – 4 in) wide, depending on the size of the chair, including a 1 cm (½ in) seam allowance on either side.

The instructions given below are for a seat cushion measuring 40 cm x 37 cm (15¾ in x 14½ in).

A PRETTY FLORAL SEAT CUSHION AND BACKREST

REQUIREMENTS
Paper template
40 cm x 37 cm (15¾ x 14½ in)
    printed fabric for cushion front
Two 37 cm x 25 cm (14½ in x
    10 in) pieces of printed fabric
    for cushion back
2.85 m x 9 cm-wide (3 yd x
    3½ in-wide) white fabric for frill
Two 1 m x 14 cm (1⅛ yd x
    5½ in) pieces of plain fabric
    for ties
40 cm x 37 cm x 2.5 cm-thick
    (15¾ in x 14½ in x 1 in-thick)
    foam rubber
Embroidery thread
Metallic thread or floss
Polyester cotton thread to
    match fabric
Stitch sealant (see page 19)
Clear glue

METHOD

1. Using the template, cut out the fabric for the cushion front and back. Cut out the foam rubber for the cushion.

2. Apply glue to edge of foam rubber. Allow to dry for a few seconds before pressing top and bottom together to give a rounded effect (see Fig. 2).

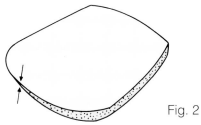

Fig. 2

3. Finish one long edge of both pieces of fabric for the back of the cushion using three-thread overlocking. Turn edge back 1 cm (½ in) and, using the sewing machine, sew with a straight stitch.

4. With RS together and using three-thread overlocking, join the short edges of the long fabric strip for the frill to form a circle.

5. Finish the long edge of the frill using **narrow hem with metallic thread** (see page 15).

6. **Gather** frill **over embroidery thread** (see page 16).

7. With RS together, pin frill to fabric for cushion front.

8. With RS together, pin raw edges of back panels to raw edges of cushion front and frill.

9. Using four-thread overlocking and starting anew at each corner, sew round edges of cushion front and frill.

10. Turn cushion cover right side out and insert foam rubber.

11. Finish all round edges of fabric for ties using **narrow hem with metallic thread** (see page 15). Secure ends with stitch sealant.

12. Position ties on the underside of the seat cushion and pin and secure by hand (see Fig. 3). Tie fabric into a bow around chair frame.

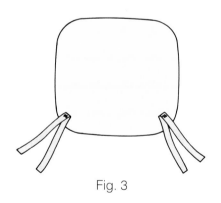

Fig. 3

BACK REST CUSHION AND COVER

To make a pattern for the back rest cushion, place tracing paper or paper over the back of the chair and trace the outline to make a template, adding a 1 cm (½ in) seam allowance right round if not adding a frill.

For the frill, measure the outer edge of the back rest and multiply by 2½ – 3. Cut the frill 8 – 10 cm (3¼ – 4 in) wide, including a 1 cm (½ in) seam allowance on either side.

The instructions given below are for a back rest cushion measuring 37 cm x 20 cm (14½ in x 8 in).

REQUIREMENTS
Paper template
37 cm x 20 cm (14½ in x 8 in) printed fabric for cushion front
Two 37 cm x 25 cm (14½ in x 10 in) pieces of printed fabric for cushion back
2.85 m x 9 cm-wide (3¼ yd x 3½ in-wide) white fabric for frill
Two 1 m x 1.5 – 2.5 cm-wide (1⅛ yd x ¾ – 1 in-wide) satin ribbons for ties
37 cm x 20 cm x 2.5 cm-thick (14½ in x 8 in x 1 in-thick) foam rubber
Embroidery thread
Metallic thread or floss
Polyester cotton thread to match fabric
Clear glue

METHOD
1. Use the template to cut out the fabric for the back rest cushion front and back and the foam rubber.

2. Apply glue to edges of foam rubber. Allow to dry for a few seconds before pressing top and bottom together to give a rounded effect (see Fig. 2).

3. Finish one edge of both pieces of fabric for the back of the back rest with three-thread overlocking. Turn edge back 1 cm (½ in) and, using the sewing machine, sew with a straight stitch.

4. With RS together and using three-thread overlocking, join short edges of fabric strip for frill to form a circle.

5. Finish frill edge using **narrow hem with metallic thread** (see page 15).

6. **Gather** frill **over embroidery thread** (see page 16).

7. With RS together, pin frill to fabric for cushion front.

8. With RS together, pin raw edges of back panels to raw edges of the back rest cushion front and frill.

9. Using four-thread overlocking and starting anew at each corner, sew all round edges.

10. Turn cushion cover right side out and insert foam rubber.

11. Position ribbon on the underside of the back rest cushion. Pin and secure by hand. Tie ribbon into a bow around chair frame.

TABLE-CLOTH

For a square and rectangular table, measure the diameter of the table and twice the fall. The fall can extend to the floor or onto your lap.

CALCULATING THE AMOUNT OF FABRIC REQUIRED
For a dinner table the cloth is usually measured to your lap, which means a fall of 15 – 20 cm (6 – 8 in), including a 1 cm (½ in) hem allowance on either side for a **narrow hem** or decorative edge using the overlocker.

JOINING THE FABRIC
If the diameter of your table-cloth is wider than the fabric width, the fabric will need to be joined to obtain the correct width. Join a strip of fabric along one or both sides of the centre piece to avoid a seam running down the centre of the cloth.

REQUIREMENTS
Fabric for table-cloth as measured
Metallic thread or floss
Polyester cotton thread to match fabric
Stitch sealant (see page 19)

METHOD
1. If necessary, join fabric along one or both sides of the centre piece to obtain the correct diameter.

2. Finish edges of table-cloth using **narrow hem with metallic thread or floss** (see page 15), or using **three-thread overlocking with metallic thread or floss** (see page 13).

3. Sew to end of fabric and chain off (see page 10), starting anew at each corner. Cut ends and apply stitch sealant.

NAPKINS

A completed napkin measures approximately 40 cm x 40 cm (15¾ in x 15¾ in). The edges of the napkins can be finished using a **narrow hem** (see pages 14 and 15), a gathered frill or gathered lace (see this page) or they can be bound (see this page).

NAPKINS WITH NARROW HEM

REQUIREMENTS
For each napkin:
40 cm x 40 cm (15¾ in x 15¾ in) plain or printed fabric for napkin
Metallic thread or floss
Polyester cotton thread to match fabric
Stitch sealant (see page 19)

METHOD
1. Finish the edges of each napkin using **narrow hem with metallic thread or floss** (see page 15), starting anew at each corner.

2. Cut ends and apply stitch sealant to secure the ends.

NAPKINS WITH BOUND EDGE

REQUIREMENTS
For each napkin:
40 cm x 40 cm (15¾ in x 15¾ in) plain or printed fabric
1.7 m x 4 cm-wide (1⅞ yd x 1½ in-wide) pre-cut bias binding in contrasting colour
Polyester cotton thread to match fabric

METHOD
1. Sew bias binding around edges of napkin using **bias binder with chain stitch** (see page 9).

NOTE: If you do not have a five-thread overlocker, sew the bias binding onto the fabric using the binder attachment on your sewing machine.

NAPKINS WITH GATHERED FRILL OR LACE

REQUIREMENTS
For each napkin:
36 cm x 36 cm (14 x 14 in) plain or printed fabric for napkin
2.85 m x 6 cm-wide (3¼ yd x 2¼ in-wide) printed or contrasting fabric for frill
OR
2.85 m x 5 – 6 cm-wide (3¼ yd x 2 – 2¼ in-wide) broderie anglaise
Metallic thread or floss
Polyester cotton thread to match fabric
Marking pen
Stitch sealant (see page 19)

METHOD
1. If using fabric instead of lace for the frill, join strips of fabric using three-thread overlocking to obtain the required length.

2. Finish the long edge of the frill using **narrow hem with metallic thread or floss** (see page 15).

3. Fold back short edges of fabric or lace 1 cm (½ in) and sew, using a sewing machine and straight stitch.

4. To shape the corners, place a small plate on the corners of each napkin, trace the outline and cut round.

5. **Gather** frill or lace to napkin **with differential feed** (see page 16). Secure ends with stitch sealant.

NOTE: If your overlocker does not have a differential feed, **gather** the frill or lace **over embroidery thread** (see page 16). With RS together, pin the frill or lace to the napkin and sew all round using three- or four-thread overlocking.

PLACEMATS

A placemat usually measures 45 cm x 30 cm (17¾ in x 12 in) and may be rectangular or oval.

The edges of the placemats may be finished off with decorative stitching using the overlocker (see pages 11 – 18); a gathered frill or lace or bound with bias binding (see page 10 on how to make your own bias binding) in a contrasting colour.

The fabric for the front of the placemat may be replaced by ready-quilted fabric (in which case omit the batting), or you can join strips of printed and plain fabric. A 1 cm (½ in) seam allowance is included in the measurements.

PLACEMATS WITH DECORATIVE STITCHING

REQUIREMENTS
For each placemat:
45 cm x 30 cm (17¾ in x 12 in) printed fabric for front
45 cm x 30 cm (17¾ in x 12 in) plain fabric for back
45 cm x 30 cm (17¾ in x 12 in) placemat batting
OR
45 cm x 30 cm (17¾ in x 12 in) ready-quilted printed fabric

For each napkin holder:
50 cm x 1 cm-wide (19½ in x ½ in-wide) ribbon
OR
50 cm (19½ in) plaited cord made with overlocker (see page 17)
Embroidery thread or metallic thread or floss
Polyester cotton thread to match fabric
Stitch sealant (see page 19)

A CHOICE OF PLACEMATS – WITH BOUND EDGE AND WITH FAGGOTING AND FRILL

METHOD

1. If not using ready-quilted fabric, place batting between the WS of the front and back of the placemat.

2. Pin and tack raw edges, working from the centre to the outside edges of the placemat.

3. Pin the ribbon or **plaited cord** (see page 17) for the napkin holder diagonally across the bottom lefthand corner of the placemat (see Fig. 4).

Fig. 4

4. Sew **three-thread wide overlocking with embroidery thread** (see page 14), or **metallic thread or floss** (see page 13) round the edges of the ready-quilted or tacked fabric.

5. Work threads away and secure ends with stitch sealant.

PLACEMATS WITH FAGGOTING AND FRILLED EDGE

A 1 cm (½ in) seam allowance has been included in the measurements for the placemat and the frill as well as for the faggoting.

REQUIREMENTS
For each placemat:
Two 30 cm x 11 cm (12 in x
    4¼ in) strips of printed fabric
Two 30 cm x 11 cm (12 in x
    4¼ in) strips of plain fabric
    colour 1
One 30 cm x 11 cm (12 in x
    4¼ in) strip of plain fabric
    colour 2
3 m x 6 cm-wide (3¼ yd x
    2¼ in-wide) plain fabric colour
    2 for frill (measuring twice the
    circumference of the placemat)

OR
3 m x 5 – 6 cm-wide (3¼ yd x
    2 – 2½ in-wide) broderie
    anglaise (twice the
    circumference of the placemat)
45 cm x 30 cm (17¾ in x 12 in)
    plain fabric for back
45 cm x 30 cm (17¾ in x 12 in)
    placemat batting
Embroidery thread
Metallic thread
Polyester cotton thread to
    match fabric

METHOD

1. Join strips of printed and plain fabric using **faggoting** (see page 17). Press.

2. If using broderie anglaise, **gather** lace to front of placemat, using **differential feed** (see page 7), keeping the placemat on top.

3. If not using broderie anglaise for frill, join short edges of fabric strips for frill, RS together, to form a circle, using

43

three-thread overlocking. Finish edge of frill using **narrow hem with metallic thread** (see page 14). **Gather** frill **over embroidery thread** (see page 16). With RS together, pin frill to front of placemat.

4. With RS together, pin back of placemat to front and frill.

5. Pin placemat batting on top of the back of the placemat.

6. Sew all round the edges using four- or five-thread overlocking.

7. Undo 7 cm (2¾ in) of the overlocking by cutting and pulling on the needle threads.

8. Turn placemat right side out and slip-stitch the opening by hand.

PLACEMATS WITH BOUND EDGE

REQUIREMENTS
For each placemat:
45 cm x 30 cm (17¾ in x 12 in) printed fabric for front
45 cm x 30 cm (17¾ in x 12 in) plain fabric for back
45 cm x 30 cm (17¾ in x 12 in) placemat batting
OR
45 cm x 30 cm (17¾ in x 12 in) ready-quilted printed fabric
1.7 m x 4 cm-wide (1⅞ yd x 1½ in-wide) pre-cut bias binding in contrasting colour (see page 10)

For each napkin holder:
50 cm x 1 cm-wide (19½ in x ½ in-wide) ribbon
OR
50 cm (19½ in) plaited cord made with overlocker (see page 17)
Polyester cotton thread to match fabric

METHOD
1. If not using ready-quilted fabric, place batting between WS of front and back of placemat.

2. Pin and tack raw edges together, working from the centre to the outside edges of the placemat.

3. Pin ribbon or plaited cord diagonally across bottom lefthand corner of ready-quilted or tacked fabric.

4. Using **bias binder with chain stitch** (see page 9), bind raw edges.

NOTE: If you do not have a five-thread overlocker, sew the bias binding using the binder attachment on your sewing machine.

PLATE WARMER

This is a wonderful way of keeping hot plates warm. This plate warmer has been designed to accommodate four dinner plates measuring 28 cm (11 in) in diameter.

To make a plate warmer for your plates, cut out a paper template measuring 2 cm (¾ in) larger than the plate.

REQUIREMENTS
Five 32 cm x 32 cm (12½ in x 12½ in) pieces of printed fabric for front
Five 32 cm x 32 cm (12½ in x 12½ in) pieces of plain fabric for back
Five 32 cm x 32 cm (12½ in x 12½ in) pieces of placemat batting
OR
Five 32 cm x 32 cm (12½ in x 12½ in) pieces ready-quilted printed fabric
5.5 m x 4 cm-wide (6 yd x 1½ in-wide) pre-cut bias binding in plain colour
Polyester cotton thread to match fabric

METHOD
1. Using the template, cut out five circles from the ready-quilted fabric, if using, or five circles from each of the fabrics for the front and the back and five circles from the batting.

TWO VARIATIONS OF TRAYCLOTH – WITH FRILL AND WITH LACE DECORATION

2. If you are not using ready-quilted fabric, pin and tack a circle of batting between a front and back fabric circle, with WS together.

3. Using pre-cut bias binding and **bias binder with chain stitch** (see page 9), bind the edge of each ready-quilted fabric circle, if using, or the raw edges of the tacked fabric circles.

NOTE: If you do not have a five-thread overlocker, sew the bias binding using the binder attachment on your sewing machine.

4. Fold first plate warmer double and mark the fold with a pin 1 cm (½ in) from the edge on either side. Position first plate warmer on top of second plate warmer. Using sewing machine and starting from the pin, sew 2 cm (¾ in) diagonally to the left, ending at the outer edge (see Fig. 5).

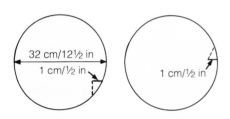

Fig. 5

5. Pin the third plate warmer to the second plate warmer on either side and, using sewing machine and starting 1 cm (½ in) from the edge, sew 2 cm (¾ in) diagonally to the right, ending at the outer edge.

6. Pin the fourth plate warmer to the third plate warmer and repeat step 4.

7. Pin the fifth plate warmer to the fourth plate warmer and repeat step 5.

TRAYCLOTH

Measure the inside of your tray to determine the size of the completed traycloth. The instructions given below are for a traycloth measuring 40 cm x 30 cm (15¾ in x 12 in).

NOTE: Remember that you will be decorating the traycloth with flatlocking, pintucks and faggoting, and that it is important always to cut the fabric larger than the size required to allow for the decorative stitchings as they are all sewn onto a fold. Cut the traycloth to size once the decorative stitching has been completed.

TRAYCLOTH WITHOUT FRILL

REQUIREMENTS
45 cm x 32 cm (17¾ in x 12½ in) plain fabric
1 m x 3 cm-wide (1⅛ yd x 1¼ in-wide) broderie anglaise
Embroidery or ribbon thread
Metallic thread
Polyester cotton thread to match fabric
Marking pen
Stitch sealant (see page 19)

METHOD

1. Using the marking pen, draw six lines 5 cm (2 in) apart on the fabric for the traycloth.

2. Position and pin the lace onto fabric as shown (see Fig. 6).

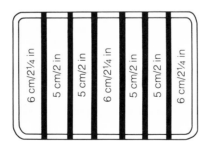

Fig. 6

3. Fold the fabric double and, keeping the lace on top, sew using **flatlocking with metallic thread** (see page 11).

4. On remaining two lines sew **flatlocking with embroidery or ribbon thread** (see page 12). Press.

5. Finish the edges of the traycloth using **three-thread overlocking with metallic thread** (see page 11), starting anew at each corner.

6. Secure ends with stitch sealant.

TRAYCLOTH WITH FRILL

REQUIREMENTS
42 cm x 32 cm (16½ in x 12½ in) plain fabric
50 cm x 3 cm-wide (19½ in x 1¼ in-wide) broderie anglaise
2.8 m x 6 cm-wide (3 yd x 2¼ in-wide) plain or printed fabric for frill
Metallic thread
Polyester cotton thread to match fabric
Marking pen

METHOD

1. Pin the lace to the front of the traycloth, positioning it diagonally across the bottom left- and top righthand corners as shown (see Fig. 7).

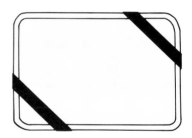

Fig. 7

2. Fold the fabric double, WS together, and keeping lace on top, sew on the lace using **flatlocking with metallic thread** (see page 11).

3. Using a marking pen, draw a line in both corners on the WS of the fabric 3 cm (1¼ in) from the stitching of lace.

4. Fold the fabric double, RS together, and sew **ladder stitch with metallic thread** (see page 12) on these lines.

5. If necessary, join strips of fabric for the frill, using three-thread overlocking, to obtain the required length.

A TEA COSY SHOWING FLATLOCKING OVER RIBBON

6. Finish frill edge using **narrow hem with metallic thread** (see page 15).

7. Turn short edges of frill back 1 cm (½ in) and hem, using sewing machine and straight stitch.

8. **Gather** frill to traycloth **with gathering attachment** (see page 9).

NOTE: If you do not have a gathering attachment, **gather** frill **over embroidery thread** (see page 16). With RS together, pin frill to traycloth and sew all round, using three- or four-thread overlocking.

TEA COSY

The instructions given below are for a tea cosy measuring 28 cm (11 in) high by 34 cm (13½ in) wide (see page 47 for pattern), including a 1 cm (½ in) seam allowance.

REQUIREMENTS
Dressmakers' tracing paper
40 cm x 28 cm (15¾ in x 11 in) plain fabric for front
34 cm x 28 cm (13½ in x 11 in) printed fabric for back
Two 34 cm x 28 cm (13½ in x 11 in) pieces of white fabric for lining
Two 34 cm x 28 cm (13½ in x 11 in) pieces of thick wadding
1.4 m x 3 cm-wide (1½ yd x 1¼ in-wide) broderie anglaise
Embroidery or ribbon thread
Metallic thread
Polyester cotton thread to match fabric
Marking pen
Stitch sealant (see page 19)

METHOD
1. Enlarge the pattern for the tea cosy on page 47 and use the dressmakers' tracing paper to cut out a template.

2. Using the template, cut out the back, the two pieces of lining and the two pieces of wadding. Remember to cut the front 3 cm (1¼ in) larger than the template around the curved edge to allow for decorative sewing.

3. Using the marking pen, draw lines 5 cm (2 in) apart on the plain fabric for the front as shown (see Fig. 8).

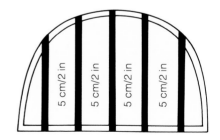

Fig. 8

4. Sew **flatlocking over ribbon with metallic thread or floss** (see page 12) on centre marked line.

5. On marked lines on either side of centre, cut fabric and fold raw edges back 1 cm (½ in) and press.

6. With RS together, sew using **faggoting with metallic thread** (see page 17) on folded edges.

7. On marked lines on either side of the faggoting, sew **flatlocking with embroidery or ribbon thread** (see page 12). Pull the stitching open to lie flat, and press.

8. Place front of tea cosy on template and cut to size.

9. Pin wadding to fabric for front and back of tea cosy.

10. **Gather** lace **over embroidery thread** (see page 16).

11. With RS together, pin lace to the front, starting 2 cm (¾ in) from the bottom edge, around the curved edge, and ending 2 cm (¾ in) from the other bottom edge (see Fig. 9).

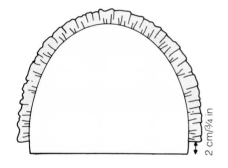

Fig. 9

12. With RS together, pin back to front.

13. Sew along curved edge, using four- or five-thread overlocking. Turn tea cosy right side out.

14. With RS together, pin and sew lining around curved edge, using four- or five-thread overlocking.

15. With WS together, insert lining into tea cosy.

16. Finish bottom edge using **three-thread wide overlocking with metallic thread** (see page 13 and Fig. 9).

17. Secure ends with stitch sealant.

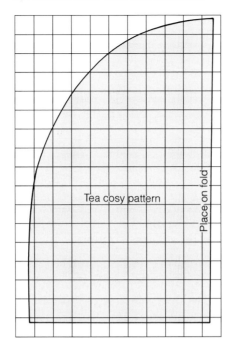

Tea cosy pattern

Place on fold

POT HOLDER

REQUIREMENTS
1 m x 18 cm (1⅛ yd x 7 in) printed fabric
Two 25 cm x 18 cm (10 in x 7 in) pieces of white fabric
Two 22 cm x 18 cm (8¾ in x 7 in) pieces of plain fabric
Two 40 cm x 18 cm (15¾ in x 7 in) pieces of placemat batting
3 m x 4 cm-wide (3¼ yd x 1½ in-wide) bias binding in plain fabric (optional)
Metallic thread or floss
Polyester cotton thread to match fabric

METHOD
1. Fold placemat batting in half. Pin white fabric on top of batting and fold back 5 cm (2 in) at the top (see Fig. 10).

Fold over

Fig. 10

2. Pin the batting on RS of printed fabric at both ends.

3. Finish edges of plain fabric for the front pockets using **three-thread wide overlocking with metallic thread or floss** (see page 13).

4. With RS together, pin front pockets on top of white fabric at both ends, and round the corners (see Fig. 11).

Fig. 11

5. Finish all round edges of pot holder using **three-thread wide overlocking with metallic thread or floss** (see page 13). Alternatively, sew bias binding around edges using **bias binder with chain stitch** (see page 9).

NOTE: If you do not have a five-thread overlocker, sew the bias binding using the bias binder attachment on your sewing machine.

PEG BAG

REQUIREMENTS
Dressmakers' tracing paper
50 cm x 40 cm (20½ in x 15¾ in) printed fabric for front
50 cm x 40 cm (20½ in x 15¾ in) plain fabric for back
60 cm x 18 – 20 cm-wide (23½ in x 7 – 8 in-wide) broderie anglaise for frill
Metallic thread or floss
Polyester cotton thread to match fabric
Small wooden coat hanger

METHOD
1. Enlarge the pattern on page 48 onto tracing paper to measure 23 cm (9 in) including a 1 cm (½ in) seam allowance, and cut out the template.

2. Place template on fabric and cut out front and back.

3. With WS of lace to RS of printed fabric, gather lace to top edge of bottom half of the peg bag using **gathering attachment** (see page 9) or using **gathering with differential feed** (see page 16).

4. With RS together, join top and bottom halves of front using four- or five-thread overlocking.

5. Finish edge of opening using **three-thread overlocking with metallic thread or floss** (see page 13).

6. With WS together, pin front to back and sew all round using **three-thread wide overlocking with metallic thread or floss** (see page 13).

7. Insert the coat hanger and fill the bag with clothes pegs.

APPLIANCE COVERS

It is very easy to make your own patterns for all your kitchen appliances.

CALCULATING THE AMOUNT OF FABRIC REQUIRED

Each cover consists of two sides plus a panel which runs across the top and down the sides. Make your own template by placing a piece of cardboard behind the appliance and tracing the outline onto the cardboard. Add 2 cm (¾ in) on either side for ease, plus a 1 cm (½ in) seam allowance around the two sides and the top edge. Add a 1 cm (½ in) seam allowance at the bottom.

After cutting out the template, measure the two sides and the top of the template. This will be the measurement for the long panel (side panel) running over the appliance. Shape the top corners as shown (see Fig. 12).

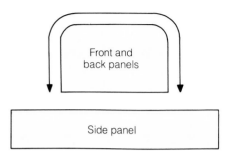

Fig. 12

The width of the side panel will depend on the width of the appliance. Measure the appliance across its widest part and add 3 cm (1¼ in) on either side for ease and for the seam allowance.

AN ATTRACTIVE BAG TO HOLD CLOTHES PEGS

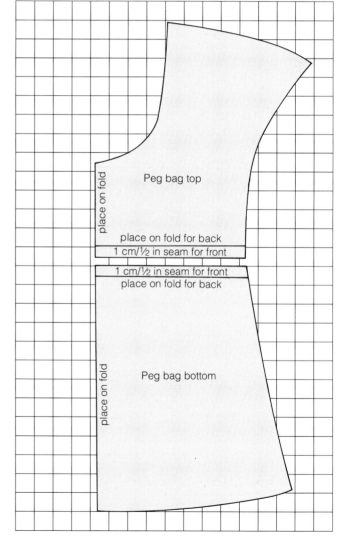

TOASTER COVER

The instructions given below are for a toaster cover measuring approximately 26 cm x 18 cm (10¼ in x 7 in), including a 1 cm (½ in) seam allowance.

REQUIREMENTS
Two 28 cm x 20 cm (11 in x 8 in) pieces of ready-quilted fabric for front and back panels
70 cm x 12 cm (27½ in x 4¾ in) piece of ready-quilted fabric for side panel
1.5 m x 4 cm-wide (1⅝ yd x 1½ in-wide) pre-made bias binding in plain fabric
1.5 m (1⅝ yd) nylon cord for piping
Metallic thread
Polyester cotton thread to match fabric
Stitch sealant (see page 19)

METHOD
1. Insert nylon cord in bias binding and, using the sewing machine, sew with straight stitch and zipper foot as closely to the cord as possible.

2. Sew the piping onto the side and top edges, excluding the bottom edge, of the front and back panels of the toaster cover (see Fig. 13).

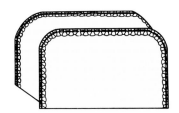

Fig. 13

3. With RS together, pin front and back panels to the side panel and sew, using four- or five-thread overlocking.

4. Finish the bottom edge of the toaster cover using **three-thread wide overlocking with metallic thread** (see page 13).

5. Secure ends with stitch sealant.

A TOASTER COVER MADE WITH READY-QUILTED FABRIC

FOOD PROCESSOR COVER

Use a template to make the cover according to the shape of the food processor, or make a cover measuring 38 cm (15 in) square, including a 1 cm (½ in) seam allowance.

REQUIREMENTS
Two 40 cm (15¾ in) square pieces of ready-quilted fabric for front and back panels
120 cm x 30 cm (1⅜ yd x 12 in) ready-quilted fabric for side panel
3 m x 4 cm-wide (3¼ yd x 1½ in-wide) pre-made bias binding in plain fabric
3 m (3¼ yd) nylon cord for piping
Metallic thread
Polyester cotton thread to match fabric
Stitch sealant (see page 19)

METHOD
1. Insert nylon cord in bias binding and, using sewing machine and zipper foot, sew as closely as possible to the cord.

2. Sew piping along side and top edges, excluding the bottom edge, of the front and back panels (see Fig. 14).

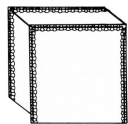

Fig. 14

3. With RS together, pin front and back panels to side panel and sew, using four- or five-thread overlocking.

4. Finish the bottom edge of the cover using **three-thread wide overlocking with metallic thread** (see page 13). Secure ends with stitch sealant.

BATHROOM

This bathroom has been decorated in plain candy pink and blue fabrics combined with a floral fabric. Notice how the floral fabric hs been used throughout the bathroom – in the towels, face-cloth, bath mat, toilet seat cover and mat as well as in the toilet roll holders.

Plain white bath and guest towels make excellent gifts when decorated with lace and ribbon.

AUSTRIAN OR FESTOON BLINDS

An Austrian or festoon blind is gathered lengthwise and across. Use an Austrian blind in conjunction with a curtain or on its own. A frill at the bottom or right around the blind makes it even more attractive. Should you decide to make a frill, use a plain rather than a printed fabric for the blind itself and a printed fabric only for the frill.

The Austrian blind is sewn onto curtain tape and can be pleated or gathered. The minimum length for a raised blind is 50 cm (19 in).

CALCULATING THE AMOUNT OF FABRIC REQUIRED

To calculate the amount of fabric, measure the width of the window and multiply by 2. Add on 2 cm (¾ in) on either side for seam allowances. For the length, measure the height of the window and multiply by 2½. Add on a seam allowance of 10 cm (4 in) at the top and 2 cm (¾) at the bottom if using a frill, or 10 – 15 cm (4 – 6 in) if not using a frill.

To calculate the amount of fabric for the frill, measure the width of the window plus twice the height of the window and multiply by 2.

To calculate the amount of heading tape required, measure the length of the rod or track and multiply by 2.

To calculate the amount of gathering tape required, measure the length of the fabric and multiply by 4.

REQUIREMENTS
Plain fabric for blind as measured
10 cm-wide (4 in-wide) strips of printed fabric for frill as measured
3 cm-wide (1¼ in-wide) strips of plain fabric for tape, measuring the length of the frill
Gathering tape as calculated
Heading tape as calculated
Polyester cotton thread to match fabric
Nylon cord measuring four times the height of the window
30 – 40 small metal rings

METHOD

1. Starting 3 cm (1¼ in) from each side edge of the fabric for the blind, sew gathering tape on lengthwise, positioning each strip 40 cm – 45 cm (15¾ in – 17¾ in) apart (see Fig. 1).

2. Fold top edge of the blind back 10 cm (4 in) and, using sewing machine and straight stitch, sew on heading tape 4 cm (1½ in) from the edge (see Fig. 1).

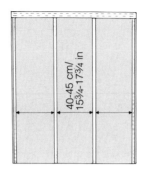

40-45 cm/ 15¾-17¾ in

Fig. 1

3. If necessary, join strips of fabric for frill and strips of fabric for tape, using three- or four-thread overlocking to obtain the required length.

4. Using overlocker and **tape guide** (see page 9), sew tape to frill.

> NOTE: If you do not have a tape guide, or cannot fit one on your overlocker, fold the tape in half, RS together, and sew, using three- or four-thread overlocking.

5. **Gather** frill to curtain along sides and bottom using **gathering attachment** (see page 9).

> NOTE: If you do not have or cannot fit a gathering attachment to your overlocker, **gather** the frill **over embroidery thread** (see page 16).

6. Insert metal rings in gathering tape 30 cm (12 in) apart. Thread nylon cord through rings and take across to one side of the blind (see Fig. 2). Pull nylon cord up to form gathers and knot cords.

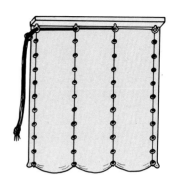

Fig. 2

DECORATED TOWELS

Bath and guest towels as well as face-cloths can be prettily decorated with broderie anglaise, ribbon and a variety of printed fabric.

BATH TOWEL

REQUIREMENTS
75 cm-wide (29½ in-wide) white or plain-coloured bath towel
75 cm x 12 cm-wide (29½ in x 4½ in-wide) printed fabric
75 cm x 12 cm-wide (29½ in x 4½ in-wide) broderie anglaise
75 cm x 25 mm-wide (29½ in x 1 in-wide) satin ribbon
Embroidery thread
Metallic thread
Polyester cotton thread to match fabric

METHOD

1. Position and pin lace 27 cm (10½ in) from the bottom of the towel. Pin ribbon to overlap raw edge of lace. Fold ribbon under at ends (see Fig. 3).

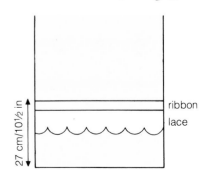

27 cm/10½ in

ribbon
lace

Fig. 3

2. Sew ribbon and lace to towel using **chain stitch with metallic thread** (see page 18). Finish ends by hand.

NOTE: If you do not have a five-thread overlocker, fold the towel and, keeping the ribbon and lace on top, sew ribbon and lace onto towel using **flatlocking with metallic thread** (see page 11).

---

3. Measure 35 cm (13¾ in) from the bottom of the towel and pin the printed fabric in position (see Fig. 4). Fold the towel and, keeping fabric on top, sew both long edges of printed fabric onto towel using **flatlocking with embroidery thread** (see page 12). Finish ends by hand.

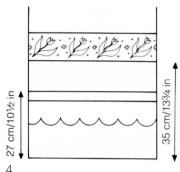

Fig. 4

GUEST TOWEL

REQUIREMENTS
55 cm-wide (21½ in-wide) white or plain-coloured guest towel
55 cm x 12 cm-wide (21½ in x 4¾ in-wide) printed fabric
55 cm x 12 cm-wide (21½ in x 4¾ in-wide) broderie anglaise
55 cm x 2.5 cm-wide (21½ in x 1 in-wide) satin ribbon
Embroidery thread
Metallic thread
Polyester cotton thread to match fabric

METHOD
1. Position and pin on the lace 20 cm (8 in) from the bottom of the towel. Pin on the ribbon to overlap raw edge of lace, folding ribbon under at ends.

---

2. Sew ribbon and lace to towel using **chain stitch with metallic thread** (see page 18). Finish ends by hand.

NOTE: If you do not have a five-thread overlocker, fold the towel and, keeping the ribbon on top, sew on the ribbon and lace using **flatlocking with metallic thread** (see page 11).

---

3. Measure 28 cm (11 in) from the bottom of the towel and pin the printed fabric in position (see Fig. 5).

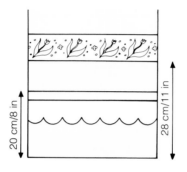

Fig. 5

4. Fold the towel, keeping fabric on top, and sew both long edges of the fabric to the towel using **flatlocking with embroidery thread** (see page 12). Finish the ends by hand.

FACE-CLOTH

REQUIREMENTS
White or plain-coloured face-cloth
30 cm x 7 cm-wide (12 in x 2¾ in-wide) printed fabric
Metallic thread
Polyester cotton thread to match fabric

METHOD
1. Position and pin the printed fabric 2 cm (¾ in) from edge.

2. Fold the face-cloth double and, keeping fabric on top, sew fabric to face-cloth using **flatlocking with metallic thread** (see page 11).

---

3. Finish all the edges of the face-cloth using **narrow hem with metallic thread** (see page 15).

BATH MAT

The instructions given below are for a bath mat measuring 70 cm x 50 cm (27½ in x 19½ in), including a 1 cm (½ in) hem allowance.

REQUIREMENTS
Two 72 cm x 12 cm (28¼ in x 4¾ in) strips of printed fabric
Two 72 cm x 12 cm (28¼ in x 4¾ in) strips of plain fabric colour 1
72 cm x 12 cm (28¼ in x 4¾ in) strip plain fabric colour 2
72 cm x 52 cm (28¼ in x 20½ in) white ready-quilted fabric for back
OR
72 cm x 52 cm (28¼ in x 22½ in) thin wadding and
72 cm x 52 cm (28¼ in x 20½ in) white fabric
Embroidery thread
Metallic thread or floss
Polyester cotton thread to match fabric
Stitch sealant (see page 19)

METHOD
1. With WS together, pin strips of printed and plain fabric together as shown (see Fig. 6).

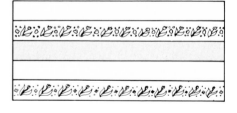

Fig. 6

2. Sew strips together using **flatlocking with embroidery thread** (see page 12). Press.

3. With WS together, pin front and back of bath mat together. (If not using ready-quilted fabric, place wadding between front and back.)

4. Finish edges of bath mat using **three-thread wide overlocking with metallic thread or floss** (see page 13). Sew the two short edges first and then the two long edges. Knot threads and secure with stitch sealant.

TOILET SEAT COVER

As shapes differ, draw a pattern of the toilet seat lid on tracing paper and add 2 cm (¾ in) all round for ease as well as the seam allowance.

REQUIREMENTS
45 cm x 40 cm (17¾ in x 15¾ in) ready-quilted printed fabric for cover
110 cm x 12 cm (1¼ yd x 4¾ in) white fabric
2.2 m x 8 cm-wide (2½ yd x 3¼ in-wide) plain fabric for frill (twice the circumference of cover)
25 cm x 4 cm-wide (10 in x 1½ in-wide) plain fabric for the bias strip
1 m (1⅛ yd) white nylon cord
Metallic thread
Polyester cotton thread to match fabric

METHOD
1. Using overlocker and **bias binder with chain stitch** (see page 9), sew bias strip to straight edge of cover.

2. If necessary, join strips of fabric for frill, using three-thread overlocking, to obtain the required length.

3. Gather frill **with gathering attachment** (see page 9) to rounded edges.

NOTE: If you do not have a gathering attachment, **gather** the frill **over embroidery thread** (see page 16).

4. Finish the two short edges and one long edge of the white fabric measuring 110 cm x 12 cm (1¼ yd x 4¾ in) using three-thread overlocking.

TOILET SEAT COVER AND MAT IN SHADES OF BLUE

5. Fold short edges back 1 cm (½ in) and sew, using sewing machine and a straight stitch. Fold the long edge which has been overlocked back 3 cm (1¼ in) to form a casing and sew using sewing machine and a straight stitch.

6. With RS together, pin raw edge of the white fabric measuring 110 cm x 12 cm (1¼ yd x 4¾ in) to the cover and sew using four- or five-thread overlocking.

7. Thread the cord through the casing (see Fig. 7), pull the cover over the toilet lid and tighten the cord until the cover fits snugly.

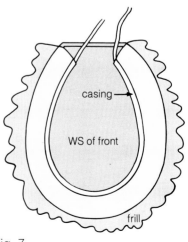

Fig. 7

TOILET MAT

REQUIREMENTS
Dressmakers' tracing paper
Two 50 cm x 11 cm (19½ in x 4¼ in) strips of printed fabric
Two 50 cm x 11 cm (19½ in x 4¼ in) strips of plain fabric colour 1
Two 50 cm x 11 cm (19½ in x 4¼ in) strips of plain fabric colour 2
50 cm x 50 cm (19½ in x 19½ in) ready-quilted fabric
3 m x 8 cm-wide (3¼ yd x 3¼ in-wide) printed fabric for frill (twice the length of the rounded edge)
20 cm x 4 cm-wide (8 in x 1½ in-wide) plain fabric for the bias strip
Embroidery thread
Floss
Metallic thread
Polyester cotton thread to match fabric
Marking pen
Stitch sealant (see page 19)

METHOD
1. Use tracing paper to cut a pattern of the toilet pedestal as illustrated.

2. With WS together, join printed and plain fabric strips, using **flatlocking with embroidery thread** as shown (see Fig. 8). Round the corners. Press on wrong side.

3. Place the traced pattern on the joined fabric strips and cut out the shape of the toilet pedestal.

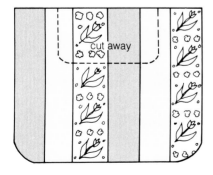

Fig. 8

4. Finish straight edges of mat with plain fabric for bias strip using **bias binder with chain stitch** (see page 9).

5. Finish pedestal edge using **three-thread wide overlocking with floss** (see page 13).

6. If necessary, join strips of fabric for frill, using three-thread overlocking, to obtain the required length.

7. **Gather** frill to toilet mat using **gathering attachment** (see page 9).

> NOTE: If you do not have a gathering attachment or cannot fit one onto your overlocker, **gather** frill **over embroidery thread** (see page 16).

8. Knot ends and finish by hand, or secure with stitch sealant.

TOILET ROLL HOLDER

A 1 cm (½ in) seam allowance is included in the measurements given below for the toilet roll holder.

REQUIREMENTS
15 cm x 15 cm (6 in x 6 in) printed ready-quilted fabric for top
82 cm x 4 cm-wide (32¼ in x 1½ in-wide) strip of plain fabric for frill
41 cm x 13 cm (16 in x 5 in) printed ready-quilted fabric for base
45 cm x 4 cm-wide (17¾ in x 1½ in-wide) plain fabric for the bias strip
Embroidery thread
Polyester cotton thread to match fabric

METHOD
1. For the top of the holder, cut out a 14 cm (5½ in) diameter circle from the square ready-quilted fabric.

2. Join the fabric strip for the frill to form a circle, using three-thread overlocking.

3. **Gather** frill **over embroidery thread** (see page 16).

4. With RS together, pin frill to ready-quilted fabric circle for top and sew, using three- or four-thread overlocking.

5. Using **bias binder with chain stitch** (see page 9), sew bias binding to one long side of ready-quilted fabric strip for base.

6. Join the short sides of the long strip using three- or four-thread overlocking.

7. With RS together, pin top to raw edge of base (see Fig. 9) and sew, using three- or four-thread overlocking.

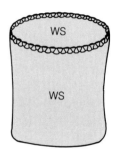

Fig. 9

TOILET ROLL HOLDER STRING

The edge of the toilet roll holder string can be finished with decorative overlocking or with a gathered frill. A 1 cm (½ in) seam allowance is included in the measurements given below.

REQUIREMENTS
1.3 m x 10 cm (1½ yd x 4 in) printed fabric
1.3 m x 10 cm (1½ yd x 4 in) plain fabric
1.3 m x 10 cm (1½ yd x 4 in) thin wadding
4.2 m x 5 cm-wide (4½ yd x 2 in-wide) plain fabric for frill (optional)
10 cm x 1 cm-wide (4 in x ½ in-wide) satin ribbon
Metallic thread or floss
Polyester cotton thread to match fabric

A HANDY BAG FOR STORING SOAPS AND A PRETTY FACE-CLOTH

SOAP BAG

This handy bag, consisting of two bags that fit into one another, is very easy to make and can be filled with soap, pot-pourri, sweets or chocolates and used as a gift or as a decoration. A 1 cm (½ in) seam allowance is included in the measurements given below.

REQUIREMENTS
30 cm x 15 cm (12 in x 6 in) printed fabric
30 cm x 15 cm (12 in x 6 in) plain fabric for lining
50 cm (19½ in) blue cord
Metallic thread or floss
Polyester cotton thread to match fabric
PVA adhesive (see page 18)
Acrylic glaze (see page 19)

METHOD

1. With WS together, sandwich the wadding between the plain and printed fabrics and pin.

2. Finish long edges using **three-thread wide overlocking with metallic thread or floss** (see page 13). Alternatively, if you prefer to finish the long edges with a frill, join fabric strips for frill to obtain the required length, then with RS together, **gather** frill to long edges **with gathering attachment** (see page 9).

NOTE: If you do not have a gathering attachment or cannot fit one onto your overlocker, **gather** frill **over embroidery thread** (see page 16).

3. Fold completed strip in half widthwise and measure 18 cm (7 in) from fold. Using sewing machine, sew across using a straight stitch. Sew another two lines, each 18 cm (7 in) apart (see Fig. 10).

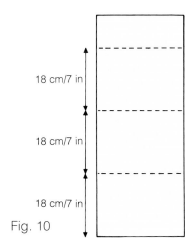

18 cm/7 in

18 cm/7 in

18 cm/7 in

Fig. 10

4. Fold ribbon in half and position raw edges on the back of the top edge of completed strip. Join short edges using **three-thread overlocking with metallic thread or floss** (see page 13).

5. Insert toilet rolls.

METHOD

1. With RS together, fold printed fabric in half widthwise, and sew one short edge and the long edge using three- or four-thread overlocking. Turn bag right side out.

2. Repeat step 1 with the lining.

3. With WS together, insert the lining into the bag.

4. Sew around the top edge of the bag using **three-thread wide overlocking with metallic thread or floss** (see page 13).

5. Paint bag with PVA adhesive.

6. Leave the bag in a warm place to dry, but before it has dried completely, shape the bag as you desire and fold the top edge back. Ensure that the bag has a solid base.

7. Once the bag is dry, paint with two to three layers of acrylic glaze, then let the bag dry again.

8. Fill the bag with small soaps, or with sweets or potpourri.

9. Tie cord around bag.

THE MAIN BEDROOM

The main bedroom is richly decorated in navy and burgundy fabrics complemented by a geometric fabric in navy, burgundy and white. Notice how the printed fabric used in the bedcover is echoed in the gathered valance and tissue box holder and how the more masculine lines of the bedcover are softened by the frilled curtains and gathered valance.

CURTAINS

CALCULATING THE AMOUNT OF FABRIC REQUIRED

Measure the window for curtains with pinch pleats and calculate the amount of fabric required (see page 28).

> **REQUIREMENTS**
> Printed fabric for curtains as measured
> 12 cm-wide (4¾ in-wide) plain fabric for frill, measuring twice the length and twice the width of curtain
> Metallic thread or floss
> Polyester cotton thread to match fabric
> Heading tape for pinch pleats
> Stitch sealant (see page 19)

METHOD

1. If necessary, join strips of fabric for frills, using three-thread overlocking, to obtain the required length.

2. Finish the edge of the frills using **narrow hem with metallic thread** (see page 15).

3. Turn the top edge of each curtain back 10 cm (4 in) and, using the sewing machine and straight stitch, sew on the heading tape 3 cm – 5 cm (1¼ in – 2 in) from the edge.

4. Finish one long edge of each curtain using three-thread overlocking.

5. Turn overlocked long edge on each curtain back 3 cm (1¼ in) and sew **flatlocked hem with metallic thread or floss** (see page 11).

6. **Gather** frill **with gathering attachment** (see page 9) to remaining long and bottom edge of each curtain.

GATHERED VALANCE

CALCULATING THE AMOUNT OF FABRIC REQUIRED

Refer to page 28 for instructions on how to calculate the amount of fabric required for a gathered valance.

> **REQUIREMENTS**
> Plain fabric for valance as measured
> 12 cm-wide (4¾ in-wide) printed fabric for frill, measuring once the length and twice the width of the valance, multiplied by 2
> Metallic thread
> Polyester cotton thread to match fabric
> Gathering tape
> Curtain hooks

METHOD

1. If necessary, join strips of fabric for valance, using three-thread overlocking, to obtain the required length.

2. Using sewing machine and straight stitch, sew strips of gathering tape lengthwise to fabric for the valance, positioning them 25 – 35 cm (10 – 13¾ in) apart (see Fig. 1).

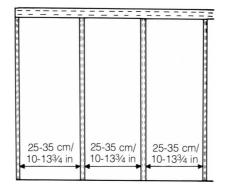

Fig. 1

3. Finish top edge of valance using three-thread overlocking.

4. Fold overlocked edge back 10 cm (4 in) and, using sewing machine and straight stitch, sew on gathering tape 3 – 5 cm (1½ – 2 in) from folded edge.

5. Join strips of printed fabric for frill, using three-thread overlocking, to obtain the required length.

6. Finish the edge of the frill using **narrow hem with metallic thread** (see page 15).

7. Fold short edges of frill back 1 cm (½ in) and sew, using sewing machine and straight stitch.

8. **Gather** frill **with gathering attachment** (see page 9) to short edges and remaining long edge of valance.

9. Attach curtain hooks to gathering tape at top edge.

10. Pull up vertically positioned gathering tape to form scallops and knot strings to secure (see Fig. 2).

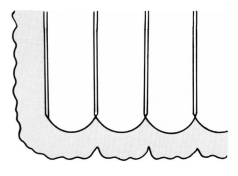

Fig. 2

PATCHWORK BEDCOVER

The instructions given below are for a bedcover measuring 240 cm x 240 cm (94½ in x 94½ in), including a 1 cm (½ in) seam allowance.

> **REQUIREMENTS**
> **For front:**
> 10 m x 40 cm (11 yd x 15¾ in) strip of printed fabric
> 9 m x 30 cm (10 yd x 12 in) strip of plain fabric colour 1
> 16 m x 10 cm (17½ yd x 4 in) strip of plain fabric colour 2
> 2.4 m x 24 cm-wide (2½ yds x 9½ in-wide) plain fabric colour 2 for top edge
>
> **For back:**
> 2.4 m x 150 cm (2½ yd x 59 in) plain fabric colour 1
> Two 2.4 m x 48 cm (2½ yd x 18¾ in) pieces of plain fabric colour 2
> 4.8 m (5¼ yds) wadding

For piping roll:
7.2 m x 20 cm-wide (8¼ yd x
   8 in-wide) plain fabric colour 2
7.2 m x 30 cm-wide (8¼ yd x
   12 in-wide) thick wadding
Polyester cotton thread to
   match fabric

METHOD

1. Place fabric for first strip on the corner of a sheet measuring 240 cm x 240 cm (94½ in x 94½ in). The sheet is used as a guide for size. Cut off excess fabric (see Fig. 3).

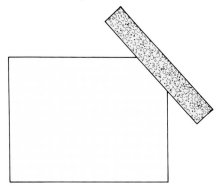

Fig. 3

2. Place second strip of fabric next to the first strip.

3. With RS together, sew the strips together using four- or five-thread overlocking (see Fig. 4). Press fabric open and cut off excess fabric.

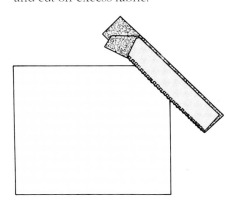

Fig. 4

4. Continue to join the remaining strips in the same way until the sheet is completely covered.

5. For the back, join a piece of plain fabric colour 2 to either side of plain fabric colour 1 using three-, four- or five-thread overlocking.

6. Join wadding using three-thread overlocking to obtain the required size.

7. Pin wadding to WS of back.

8. If necessary, join strips of fabric for piping roll using three-thread overlocking, to obtain the required length.

9. Round the bottom two corners of the bedcover (see Fig. 5).

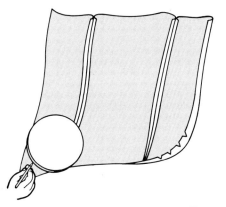

Fig. 5

10. With RS together, sew piping roll onto three sides of front of bedcover.

11. Roll thick wadding lengthwise to resemble a Swiss roll, place in piping roll and pin.

12. With RS together, pin back to front and sew all round using four- or five-thread overlocking. Turn fabric right side out.

13. Join strips of fabric for top edge of bedcover, using three-thread overlocking, to obtain the required length.

14. With RS of top edge of bedcover to back of remaining raw edge of bedcover, sew using four- or five-thread overlocking.

15. Turn top edge 12 cm (4¾ in) over to the front, fold under 1 cm (½ in) and, using sewing machine and straight stitch, close seam.

TISSUE BOX COVER

REQUIREMENTS
Two 26 cm x 13 cm (10¼ in x
   5¼ in) pieces of ready-quilted
   printed fabric for sides
Two 50 cm x 9 cm (19½ in x
   3½ in) pieces of ready-quilted
   printed fabric for top
Two 1 m x 4 cm (1⅛ yd x 1½ in)
   pieces of plain fabric for frills
Metallic thread
Polyester cotton thread to
   match fabric
Stitch sealant (see page 19)

METHOD

1. Finish edge of fabric for frills using **narrow hem with metallic thread** (see page 15).

2. Finish one long edge of each piece of ready-quilted fabric for the top, using **three-thread wide overlocking with metallic thread** (see page 13).

3. With RS together, **gather** frill **with gathering attachment** (see page 9) to remaining long edge of each top piece.

4. With RS together, pin side panel to frilled edge of each top piece.

5. Sew seam using four- or five-thread overlocking.

6. Using sewing machine and a straight stitch and with RS together, sew centre seam (overlocked edge) with a 2 cm (¾ in) seam allowance, leaving an opening of 10 cm (4 in) in the centre (see Fig. 6).

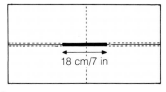

18 cm/7 in

Fig. 6

7. Finish the bottom edge of the tissue box cover using **three-thread wide overlocking with metallic thread or floss** (see page 13). Place cover over tissue box.

NURSERY

This room has been decorated in a combination of yellow and green. Once your baby has arrived, blue or pink, as the case may be, can be added. The items described in the pages to follow are both practical and attractive, and make wonderful gifts for any mother-to-be.

CURTAINS

CALCULATING THE AMOUNT OF FABRIC REQUIRED

Measure the window and calculate the amount of fabric required for curtains with pinch pleats (see page 28).

REQUIREMENTS
Floral fabric for curtains
   as measured
10 cm-wide (4 in-wide) plain
   fabric for frill, measuring twice
   the length of the curtain
Heading tape for pinch pleats
Metallic thread or floss
Polyester cotton thread to
   match fabric
Stitch sealant (see page 19)

METHOD

1. If necessary, join strips of fabric for frill, using three-thread overlocking, to obtain the required length.

2. Finish edge of frill using **narrow hem with metallic thread or floss** (see page 15).

3. **Gather** the frill to one side edge of the curtain **with gathering attachment** (see page 9). Secure ends with stitch sealant.

NOTE: If you do not have a gathering attachment or cannot fit one onto your overlocker, **gather** frill **over embroidery thread** (see page 16).

---

4. Finish the remaining side and top edge of each curtain, using three-thread overlocking.

5. Fold the side edge back 2 cm (¾ in) and sew, using sewing machine and straight stitch.

6. Fold the top edge of the curtain back 5 – 10 cm (2 – 4 in) and, using straight stitch on sewing machine, sew on the heading tape 3 – 4 cm (1¼ – 1½ in) from the edge.

7. Fold bottom edge back 5 – 10 cm (2 – 4 in) and finish using **blind hem attachment or foot** (see page 9) or straight stitch on sewing machine.

TIE-BACKS WITH ROSETTES

REQUIREMENTS
Two 60 cm x 12 cm (23½ in x
   4¾ in) pieces of printed fabric
   for fronts of tie-backs
Two 60 cm x 12 cm (23½ in x
   4¾ in) pieces of plain fabric
   for backs of tie-backs
Two 50 cm x 6 cm (19½ in x
   2¼ in) pieces of plain fabric
   for rosettes
Two 60 cm x 12 cm (23½ in x
   4¾ in) pieces of iron-on
   interfacing
Polyester cotton thread
   to match fabric
Metallic thread or floss
Four small plastic rings
Ruffler foot for sewing machine

METHOD

1. Shape tie-backs as shown (see Fig. 1).

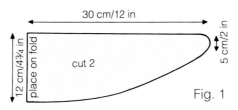

Fig. 1

2. Iron interfacing to WS of printed fabric for front of tie-backs.

3. Using ruffler foot on sewing machine, sew pleats on one long edge of fabric for rosettes. Cut 20 cm (8 in) long.

4. Arrange each piece of pleated fabric in a circle to form a rosette and, using sewing machine and straight stitch, sew to one end of tie-back.

5. With WS of tie-backs together, sew all round using **three-thread wide overlocking with metallic thread or floss** (see page 13).

6. Sew plastic rings to ends of tie-backs.

CURTAIN LINING

Curtain lining is useful in a baby's room to keep out the sun. As this curtain lining consists of two pieces of fabric of equal measurements, it can be used on its own or in conjunction with a curtain. It can be hung on spring wire or from a track on the inside of the window, or it can be fitted onto a double track or rod on the outside of the window.

CALCULATING THE AMOUNT OF FABRIC REQUIRED

To calculate the width of each curtain lining, measure the length of the track or rod, divide the measurement in half and add 15 – 20 cm (6 – 8 in) for ease plus a 2 cm (¾ in) seam allowance on either side. Measure the height of the window and add 20 cm (8 in) onto each lining for hem and seam allowances. (For example, if the width of the window recess is 1 m (1⅛ yd) and the length 2 m (2¼ yd), each curtain lining should measure about 74 cm (29 in) wide by 2.2 m (2½ yd) long.

REQUIREMENTS
White fabric for curtain lining as
   measured
12 cm-wide (4¾ in-wide) strips of
   printed fabric, equal to width
   and length measurement of
   curtain as measured
Polyester cotton thread to
   match fabric
Metallic thread or floss
Gathering tape or spring wire

METHOD

1. Measure 16 cm (6¼ in) from long edge of lining and pin WS of printed fabric to RS of white fabric (see Fig. 2).

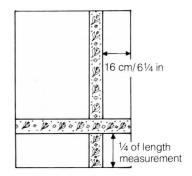

16 cm/6¼ in

¼ of length measurement

Fig. 2

2. Divide length measurement by 4 (for example, 2 m ÷ 4 = 50 cm [2¼ yd ÷ 4 = 19½ in]). Position WS of printed fabric to RS of white fabric this distance from the bottom edge.

3. Repeat the procedure (steps 1 and 2) with the other curtain lining.

> NOTE: Ensure that on both curtains, the pattern of the printed fabric runs in the same direction.

4. Sew the printed fabric onto the curtain lining using **flatlocking with metallic thread or floss** (see page 11), keeping the printed fabric on top. First sew on the horizontal strips and then the vertical strips.

> NOTE: When sewing over seams and joins, use differential feed 1.5.

5. Finish top and both side edges using three-thread overlocking.

6. Fold the sides of the curtain lining back 2 cm (¾ in) and sew, using straight stitch on sewing machine.

7. Fold bottom edge back 5 cm (2 in) and sew hem using **blind hem attachment or foot** (see page 8) or straight stitch on sewing machine.

8. If using gathering tape, fold top edge back 10 cm (4 in) and sew on tape 3 – 4 cm (1¼ – 1½ in) from the edge, using sewing machine and straight stitch. If using spring wire, fold top edge back 3 cm (1¼ in) and sew, using sewing machine and straight stitch. Insert hooks or wire.

NAPPY BAG WITH CHANGING MAT

The nappy bag, to keep toiletries and nappies to hand, is attached to the changing mat and after use folds into a easy-to-carry bag.

A 1 cm (½ in) seam allowance is included in the measurements.

REQUIREMENTS
For nappy bag:
Two 50 cm x 30 cm (29½ in x 12 in) pieces of ready-quilted printed fabric for back
OR
Two 50 cm x 30 cm (29½ in x 12 in) pieces of printed fabric for back and
Two 48 cm x 28 cm (18¾ in x 11 in) pieces of wadding
Two 74 cm x 30 cm (29¼ in x 12 in) pieces of plain fabric for front
Two 70 cm x 30 cm (27½ in x 12 in) pieces of white or yellow cotton PVC for front lining (see page 19)
Two 50 cm x 30 cm (29½ in x 12 in) pieces of white or yellow cotton PVC for back lining (see page 19)

For changing mat:
75 cm x 50 cm (29½ in x 19½ in) ready-quilted printed fabric
OR
75 cm x 50 cm (29½ in x 19½ in) printed fabric
and
73 cm x 48 cm (28¾ in x 19 in) wadding
75 cm x 50 cm (29½ in x 19½ in) white or yellow cotton PVC (see page 19)
1 m x 2.5 cm-wide (1⅛ yd x 1 in-wide) ribbon or twill band for handles
Embroidery thread
Metallic thread or floss
Polyester cotton thread to match fabric
Marking pen
Five metal press-studs or poppers

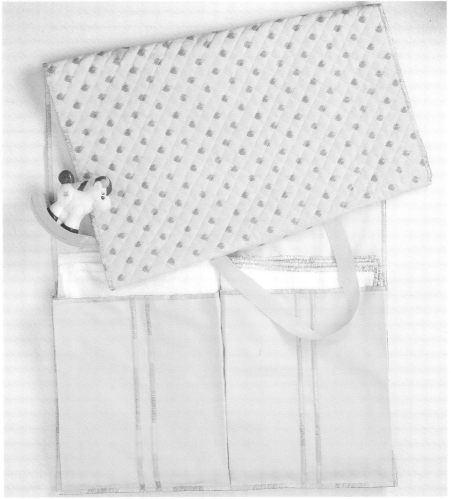

A CHANGING MAT CUM BAG FOR STORING NAPPIES AND TOILETRIES

METHOD

1. Cut ribbon or twill band in half and pin to one long side of bag back to form a handle (see Fig. 3).

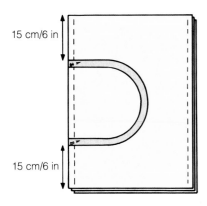

15 cm/6 in

15 cm/6 in

Fig. 3

2. Pin WS of PVC for back lining to WS of bag back.

3. Complete second bag back as above.

4. Using a marking pen, mark fold lines and lines for flatlock topstitching on bag front as shown (see Fig. 4).

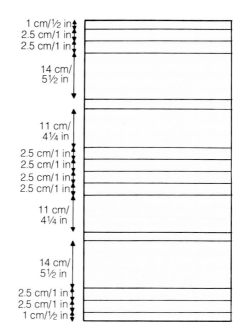

1 cm/½ in
2.5 cm/1 in
2.5 cm/1 in

14 cm/
5½ in

11 cm/
4¼ in

2.5 cm/1 in
2.5 cm/1 in

2.5 cm/1 in
2.5 cm/1 in

11 cm/
4¼ in

14 cm/
5½ in

2.5 cm/1 in
2.5 cm/1 in
1 cm/½ in

Fig. 4

5. With WS together, sew **flatlocking with metallic thread or floss** (see page 11) on marked lines.

6. Pin WS of PVC for front lining to WS of bag front.

7. Sew **three-thread wide overlocking with metallic thread or floss** (see page 13) along one long front edge, keeping fabric on top.

8. Complete second bag front as above.

9. Fold pleats on bag front as shown and pin (see Fig. 4).

10. With WS together, pin bag front to bag back, ensuring that the overlocked edge and handle are in line.

11. Keeping the bag front on top, sew the short edges and then the long edge using **three-thread wide overlocking with metallic thread or floss** (see page 13). Leave the long side with the handles open.

12. Complete second bag front and back as above.

13. Pin WS of PVC for changing mat to WS of ready-quilted fabric for changing mat or, if using fabric and wadding, sandwich the wadding between the WS of the PVC and WS of the fabric.

14. Keeping the PVC on top, finish the two long edges of the changing mat using **three-thread wide overlocking with metallic thread or floss** (see page 13).

15. Pin the back of each bag to each end of the changing mat.

16. Sew both bags to the short sides of the changing mat using **three-thread wide overlocking with metallic thread or floss** (see page 13).

17. Insert press-studs or poppers along the sides where handles are attached.

WRAP-IT-ALL PLAYMAT

The wrap-it-all padded playmat is ideal for use at home as well as when visiting. Use it to carry all your baby's toys, or as a playmat at home or on the beach. In an emergency, it can even be used as a changing mat. The mat measures 124 cm (48¾ in) in diameter, including a 1 cm (½ in) seam allowance.

A PLAYMAT THAT DOUBLES AS A BAG FOR BABY'S TOYS

METHOD

1. Fold fabric in half lengthwise and crosswise to find the centre. Using the marking pen, mark a quarter circle measuring 63 cm (24¾ in) from the centre. Cut along marked line.

2. If not using the ready-quilted fabric, sandwich the wadding between the WS of the printed and plain fabrics.

3. Sew all round using **three-thread wide overlocking with metallic thread or floss** (see page 13). Secure ends with stitch sealant.

4. Insert eyelets at 20 cm (8 in) intervals around circumference. Thread nylon cord through holes and pull up to form a bag (see Fig. 5).

Fig. 5

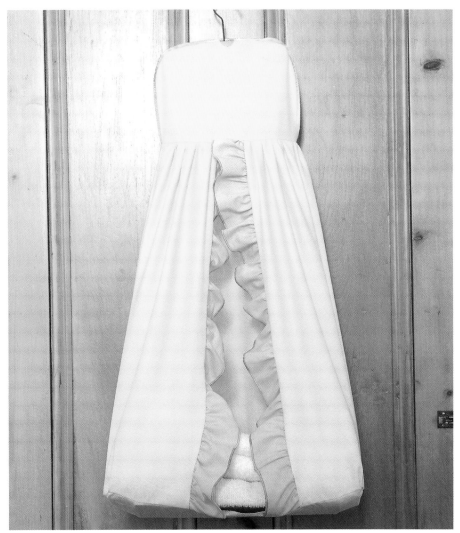

AN ATTRACTIVE FRILLED BAG FOR STORING NAPPIES

NAPPY BAG

METHOD

1. To make the frill, join strips of plain fabric in a contrasting colour, using three-thread overlocking, to obtain the required length.

2. Finish edge of frill using **narrow hem with metallic thread** (see page 15). Cut frill in half widthwise.

3. **Gather** the frill **with gathering attachment** (see page 9) to both short sides of the plain fabric for the centre section of the nappy bag.

NOTE: If you do not have a gathering attachment or cannot fit one onto your overlocker, **gather** frill **over embroidery thread** (see page 16).

4. Cut a small opening in the top section, to accommodate the hanger, and neaten the edge.

5. Round the corners of the top section. Sew along the two short sides and along the one long side of the top section using **three-thread wide overlocking with metallic thread** (see page 13 and Fig. 6).

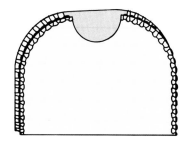

Fig. 6

6. Mark the centre of one long side of the fabric for the base of nappy bag with a pin. Starting 3 cm (1¼ in) from the centre, pin the centre section of the nappy bag to the base, folding a small pleat for ease at corners.

7. Starting anew at each corner, finish edges all round using four- or five-thread overlocking.

8. Secure ends with stitch sealant.

9. **Gather** top of centre section of nappy bag **over embroidery thread** (see page 16).

10. Pin centre section to top section of nappy bag, overlapping frills.

11. Join centre and top sections, using four- or five-thread overlocking.

12. Insert hanger, and position cardboard in the base of the nappy bag.

BABY PILLOWCASE

The instructions given below are for a pillowcase to fit an airflow pillow measuring 33 cm x 23 cm (13 in x 9 in). The measurements given include a 1 cm (½) seam allowance.

REQUIREMENTS

35 cm x 25 cm (13¾ in x 10 in) plain fabric for front
Two 25 cm x 20 cm (10 in x 8 in) pieces of plain fabric for back
2.7 m x 6 cm-wide (3 yd x 2¼-in wide) plain fabric for frill
Embroidery thread
Metallic thread
Polyester cotton thread to match fabric
Stitch sealant (see page 19)

METHOD

1. Join strips of fabric for frill to obtain the required length. With RS together, join short edges, using three-thread overlocking.

2. Finish edge of frill using **narrow hem with metallic thread or floss** (see page 15).

3. Overlock one long edge of each piece of fabric for the back of the pillowcase. Fold overlocked long edge back 1 cm (½ in) and sew, using sewing machine and straight stitch.

4. **Gather** frill **over embroidery thread** (see page 16).

5. With RS together, pin frill to pillowcase front. With RS and raw edges together, pin pillowcase backs to pillowcase front.

6. Starting anew at each corner, sew all round pillowcase using three- or four-thread overlocking.

7. Secure ends with Fray Check, and turn pillowcase right side out.

QUILT-IN-A-DAY COT QUILT

This cot quilt is quick and easy to make and is an excellent gift for a mother-to-be. It is also a good way to make use of any leftover fabric.

The instructions given below are for a quilt measuring 127 cm x 87 cm (50 in x 34¼ in). The measurements include a 1 cm (½ in) seam allowance.

REQUIREMENTS

Fourteen 18 cm (7 in) squares of printed fabric for front
Thirteen 18 cm (7 in) squares of plain fabric 1 for front
Thirteen 18 cm (7 in) squares of plain fabric 2 for front
Forty 15 cm (6 in) squares of plain fabric for back
Two 80 cm x 15 cm (31½ in x 6 in) pieces of printed fabric
Two 1.3 m x 15 cm (1½ yd x 6 in) pieces of printed fabric
1.13 m x 90 cm (1¼ yd x 35½ in) plain fabric for lining
Two 80 cm x 15 cm (31½ in x 15 in) pieces of thick wadding
Two 1.3 m x 15 cm (1½ yd x 6 in) pieces of thick wadding
Polyester filling for forty squares
Polyester cotton thread to match fabric

METHOD

1. For the front, place a larger square of fabric onto a smaller square, WS together, and sew around three sides, using three-thread overlocking, folding one tuck in each side so that edges align (see Fig. 7).

Fig. 7

2. Fill the square with polyester filling, and stitch fourth side closed using three-thread overlocking.

3. Repeat above for remaining squares.

4. Arrange squares in eight rows of five squares to form a pattern.

5. With RS together, join squares using four-thread overlocking.

6. Sew the strips of wadding to the two long and two short strips of the printed fabric, using three-thread overlocking.

BABY'S TIDY-ALL, PILLOWCASE AND QUILT-IN-A-DAY COT QUILT IN YELLOW AND GREEN

HINT
Leftover scraps of fabric can be used to make a lovely duvet for a teenager's room. Simply increase the number of squares.

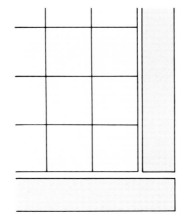

Fig. 8

7. With RS together, sew the long strips to the joined squares using four-thread overlocking (see Fig. 8). With RS together, sew the short strips to the joined squares using four-thread overlocking (see Fig. 8).

8. With RS together, pin lining to front and, using four- or five-thread overlocking, sew all round the quilt, leaving a 15 cm (6 in) gap on one side.

9. Turn the quilt right side out, and slipstitch the opening by hand.

TIDY-ALL

Keep all your baby's toiletries close at hand in this attractive tidy-all which measures 80 cm x 75 cm (31½ in x 29½ in). This measurement includes a 1.5 cm (½ in) seam allowance.

REQUIREMENTS

90 cm x 78 cm (35½ in x 30¾ in)
 plain fabric for front
80 cm x 75 cm (31½ in x 29½ in)
 plain fabric for back
27 cm x 23 cm (10½ in x 9 in)
 printed fabric for pocket No. 1
Two 35 cm x 30 cm (13¾ in x
 12 in) pieces of plain fabric for
 pockets No. 2 and 3
Two 50 cm x 4 cm (19½ in x
 1½ in) pieces of printed
 fabric for pocket frills
Two 50 cm x 6 cm (19½ in x
 2¼ in) pieces of plain fabric
 for rosettes
Two 50 cm x 6 cm (19½ in x
 2¼ in) pieces of printed fabric
 for rosettes
Four 25 cm x 20 cm (10 in x 8 in)
 pieces of printed fabric for
 the straps
80 cm x 7 cm (31½ in x 2¾ in)
 printed fabric for pin holder
80 cm x 12 cm (31½ in x 4¾ in)
 wadding for pin holder
80 cm x 75 cm (31½ in x 29½ in)
 thin wadding
1 m x 2.5 cm-wide (1¹⁄₁₀ yd x
 1 in-wide) ribbon to match
 the fabric
1 m (1¹⁄₁₀ yd) 4/6 cord elastic
 for pockets
Embroidery thread
Metallic thread
Polyester cotton thread to
 match fabric
Fusible webbing (see page 18)
Marking pen
1 m-long (1¹⁄₁₀ yd-long) wooden
 rod/dowel
Ruffler foot for sewing machine

METHOD

1. Finish edge of fabric for frill and both sides of fabric for rosettes using **narrow hem with metallic thread** (see page 15).

2. Decorate the plain fabric for pockets No. 2 and 3 using **flatlocking with metallic thread** (see page 11) and **flatlocking with embroidery thread** (see page 12). Cut pockets to measure 27 cm x 23 cm (10½ in x 9 in).

3. Thread the elastic through the **elastic gatherer attachment or foot** on your overlocker and sew the elastic and the frill to the top of all three pockets, keeping elastic on top and WS of fabric facing up (see page 8).

4. Join pockets using three- or four-thread overlocking.

5. Position the three pockets along the bottom edge of the fabric for the front of the tidy-all and, using sewing machine and straight stitch, sew the pockets onto the front (see Fig. 9).

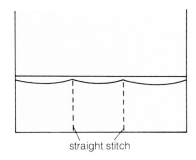

straight stitch

Fig. 9

6. Using ruffler foot on sewing machine, sew pleats on one long edge of the fabric for rosettes. Cut pleated fabric 20 cm (8 in) long.

7. Arrange pleated fabric in a circle to form a rosette and place on front of tidy-all 10 cm (4 in) from the top edge and 6 cm (2¼ in) apart. Using sewing machine, sew rosettes to tidy-all using straight stitch (see Fig. 10).

8. Using the marking pen, draw a line 28 cm (11 in) from the top of tidy-all.

9. Keeping ribbon on top, sew ribbon onto marked line using **flatlocking with metallic thread** (see page 11).

10. Using the marking pen, mark lines 35 cm (13¾ in), 39 cm (15¼ in) and 43 cm (17 in) from the top edge.

11. Sew **flatlocking with embroidery thread** (see page 12) on these three marked lines.

12. Using the marking pen, draw a line 49 cm (19¼ in) from the top.

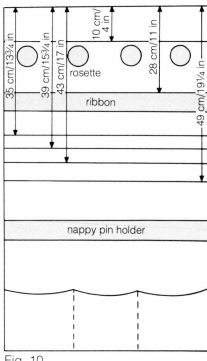

Fig. 10

13. Pin the printed fabric for the pin holder on marked line. Sew one edge only, using **flatlocking with metallic thread** (see page 11), keeping printed fabric on top.

14. Fold wadding double and place under printed fabric. Pin bottom edge of printed fabric to tidy-all and sew, using **flatlocking with metallic thread** (see page 11), keeping printed fabric on top.

15. Fold fabric for straps in half lengthwise, RS together. Sew long edge using three-thread overlocking.

16. Turn straps right side out, position seams at centre back and press.

17. Fold straps in half widthwise and pin raw edges of straps to front of top edge of tidy-all and pin.

18. With RS together, pin the back of the tidy-all to the front.

19. Pin wadding on top of back and trim edges if necessary (see Fig. 11).

20. Starting anew at each corner, sew all four sides of the tidy-all, using four- or five-thread overlocking.

A SELECTION OF PRETTY BABY'S BIBS

BABY'S BIB

The baby's bib measures 23 cm x 18 cm (9 in x 7 in) including a 1 cm (½ in) seam allowance.

REQUIREMENTS
25 cm x 20 cm (10 in x 8 in) towelling or fabric
25 cm x 20 cm (10 in x 8 in) thin PVC
1 m x 4 cm-wide (1⅛ yd x 1½ in-wide) pre-made bias binding in matching or contrasting colour
OR
1 m x 2 – 2.5 cm-wide (1⅛ yd x ¾ – 1 in-wide) satin ribbon
3 cm-wide (1¼ in-wide) lace, measuring 2½ times the circumference of the bib (optional)
Metallic thread
Polyester cotton thread to match fabric

METHOD
1. Cut bib according to the pattern as illustrated (see Fig. 13).

2. With WS together, pin PVC to towelling or fabric.

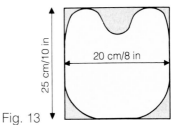

25 cm/10 in

20 cm/8 in

Fig. 13

3. Finish edges using **three-thread wide overlocking with metallic thread or floss** (see page 13).

4. If using lace, position fabric on top of lace, RS together, and gather around edges using **gathering with differential feed** (see page 16).

5. Finish neck edge with bias binding or ribbon, using **bias binder with chain stitch** (see page 9) or the bias binder attachment on sewing machine, leaving long ends at both sides to tie the bib.

NAPPIES

The instructions given below are for a nappy measuring 60 cm (23½ in) square, including a 1 cm (½ in) hem allowance.

REQUIREMENTS
61 cm (24 in) square of strong white towelling
Floss
Polyester cotton thread to match fabric
Stitch sealant (see page 19)

METHOD
1. Finish the edges of the towelling using **three-thread wide overlocking with floss** (see page 13), starting anew at each corner.

2. Secure ends with stitch sealant.

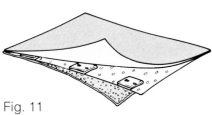

Fig. 11

21. Cut a 10 cm (4 in) slit in the back of the tidy-all (see Fig. 12) and turn tidy-all right side out. Close the slit by hand, or place a small strip of fusible webbing behind the slit and iron to close.

Fig. 12

22. Insert wooden rod through loops and hang on wall.

A LITTLE GIRL'S ROOM

Decorated in a combination of pink and green, this pretty room will gladden the heart of any little girl.

Let your daughter use fabric crayons to draw a picture on the two pieces of white fabric for the front of the continental pillowcase. The crayons are fully washable and fade proof.

The curtains are held back by tie-backs decorated with green fabric bows stiffened with PVA adhesive.

The frilled duvet cover is made up of 12 blocks, each decorated differently. Copy the ideas described on pages 75 – 77 or use your imagination to create a unique duvet cover for your little girl.

CURTAINS

CALCULATING THE AMOUNT OF FABRIC REQUIRED

Measure the window and calculate the amount of fabric required for curtains with pinch pleats (see page 28).

REQUIREMENTS
Fabric for curtain as measured
10 cm-wide (4 in-wide) fabric for
  frill, measuring twice the length
  of each curtain
Heading tape for pinch pleats
Metallic thread or floss
Polyester cotton thread to
  match fabric
Stitch sealant (see page 19)

METHOD

1. If necessary, join strips of fabric for frills, using three-thread overlocking, to obtain the required length.

2. Finish edge of fabric for frill using **narrow hem with metallic thread** (see page 15).

3. Finish one long edge and both short edges of each curtain using three-thread overlocking.

4. Fold top edge back 10 cm (4 in) and, using sewing machine and straight stitch, sew on heading tape 3 – 5 cm (1¼ – 2 in) from top edge.

5. Fold overlocked long edge of each curtain back 3 cm (1¼ in) and press.

6. Fold the fabric back again to encase the overlocked edge in the hem and sew **flatlocked hem with metallic thread or floss** (see page 13), keeping the curtain on top.

7. Fold the hem along the bottom overlocked edge of the curtain back 5 cm (2 in) and press.

8. Fold the fabric back again to encase the overlocked edge in the hem and sew **flatlocked hem with metallic thread or floss** (see page 13), keeping the curtain on top.

9. Using the **gathering attachment** (see page 9), gather the frill to the remaining long edge of the curtain. Fold the short edges of frill back 1 cm (½ in) and, using a sewing machine, sew with straight stitch.

10. Seal ends with stitch sealant.

TIE-BACKS WITH STIFFENED BOWS

REQUIREMENTS
Two 60 cm x 12 cm (23½ in x
  4¾ in) pieces of printed fabric
  for tie-back fronts
Two 60 cm x 12 cm (23½ in x
  4¾ in) pieces of plain fabric
  for tie-back backs
Two 60 cm x 12 cm (23½ in x
  4¾ in) pieces of iron-on
  interfacing
Two 70 cm x 10 cm (27½ in x
  4 in) pieces of plain fabric for
  bow streamer
Two 45 cm x 10 cm (17¾ in x
  4 in) pieces of plain fabric for
  first bow
Two 40 cm x 10 cm (15¾ in x
  4 in) pieces of plain fabric for
  second bow
Two 10 cm x 6 cm (4 in x 2¼ in)
  pieces of plain fabric for
  bow band
Metallic thread or floss
Polyester cotton thread to
  match fabric
PVA adhesive (see page 19)
Acrylic glaze (see page 19)
Wire coat hanger
Clothes pegs
Glue gun with glue sticks
Four small plastic rings

METHOD

1. Shape the fabric for the tie-backs as shown (see Fig. 1).

Fig. 1

2. Using a hot dry iron, press the iron-on interfacing to front of tie-backs.

3. With WS together, pin tie-back fronts to backs.

4. Sew all round using **three-thread wide overlocking with metallic thread or floss** (see page 13).

5. Paint PVA adhesive to one side of each piece of fabric for the streamer, first bow, second bow and bow band and fold the raw edges back towards centre back and overlap edges by 5 mm (¼ in) (see Fig. 2).

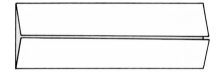

Fig. 2

6. Peg the painted wet fabric to the hanger and allow to dry for 10 – 20 minutes. Before fabric dries completely, fold short edges of first and second bows towards centre back (see Fig. 3).

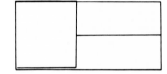

Fig. 3

7. Position first bow, then second bow, on top of streamer. Tie bow band around bow, pull tightly and glue in position. Cut a V-shape in ends of streamer. Paint both bows with two to three layers of acrylic glaze.

8. When dry, glue completed bows to front of each tie-back.

PATCHWORK DUVET COVER

The instructions given below are for a duvet cover measuring 200 cm x 150 cm (79 in x 59 in), including a 1 cm (½ in) seam allowance.

REQUIREMENTS

Four 45 cm x 40 cm (17¾ in x 15¾ in) pieces of plain fabric colour 1

Sixteen 50 cm x 10 cm (19½ in x 4 in) strips of plain fabric colour 1

Six 45 cm x 40 cm (17¾ in x 15¾ in) pieces of plain fabric colour 2

Five 1.5 m x 11 cm-wide (1⅝ yd x 4¼ in-wide) strips of printed fabric for gathering

Two 3 m x 11 cm-wide (3¼ yd x 4¼ in-wide) strips of printed fabric for gathering

Four 4 m x 11 cm-wide (4⅜ yd x 4¼ in-wide) strips of printed fabric for gathering

1.5 m x 10 cm-wide (1⅝ yds x 4 in-wide) printed fabric for facing

2 m x 1.5 m (2¼ yd x 1⅝ yd) plain fabric for back

Three 50 cm x 6 cm (19½ in x 2¼ in) pieces of printed fabric for rosettes

9 m x 10 cm-wide (10 yd x 4 in-wide) white broderie anglaise

1.5 m x 6 cm-wide (1⅝ yds x 2¼ in-wide) broderie anglaise

1 m x 5 cm-wide (1⅛ yd in x 2 in-wide) broderie anglaise

1 m x 3 cm-wide (1⅛ yd in x 1¼ in-wide) broderie anglaise

2 m x 0.5 – 1 cm-wide (2¼ yd x ¼ –½ in-wide) satin ribbon in matching colour

1.5 m x 3 mm-wide (1⅝ yds x ⅛ in-wide) satin ribbon in matching colour

Embroidery thread

Metallic thread or floss

Polyester cotton thread to match fabric

Marking pen

50 cm (19½ in) dissolving plastic (see page 19)

Four pottery buttons for Block 9

Three decorative buttons for Block 1

Five metal press-studs or poppers

Ruffler foot for sewing machine

METHOD

1. *For Block 1 – Decoration with rosettes,* finish both long edges of fabric for rosettes using **narrow hem with metallic thread** (see page 15).

2. Using ruffler foot on sewing machine, sew pleats on one long edge of the fabric for the rosettes. Cut 20 cm (8 in) long.

3. Cut one piece of plain fabric colour 2 measuring 45 cm x 40 cm (17¾ in x 15¾ in) into a 37 cm (14½ in) square.

4. Arrange rosettes on the fabric square and, using sewing machine, sew with straight stitch.

5. Position decorative buttons in centre of rosettes and sew on by hand.

6. *For Block 2 – Faggoting with metallic thread,* join eight strips of plain fabric colour 1 measuring 50 cm x 10 cm (19½ in x 4 in) using **faggoting** (see page 17).

7. Fold the fabric at a 45 degree angle and cut out a 37 cm (14½ in) square.

8. *For Block 3 – Three-thread pin-tucks with metallic thread,* draw eight parallel lines, 4 cm (1½ in) apart, on a piece of plain fabric colour 2.

9. Sew **three-thread pin-tucks** (see page 17) on marked lines.

10. Using the sewing machine, sew rows of straight stitching 6 cm (2¼ in) apart at right angles to the pin-tucks (see page 17), ensuring that the rows of stitching run alternately up and down.

11. Cut fabric into a square measuring 37 cm (14½ in).

12. *For Block 4 – Embroidery thread strings,* use a marking pen to draw three lines, 6 cm (2¼ in) apart, on a piece of plain fabric colour 1 measuring 45 cm x 40 cm (17¾ in x 15¾ in).

13. With WS together, fold fabric double and, using **three-thread wide overlocking with embroidery thread** (see page 14), sew on marked lines. Tighten the needle tension to 6 – 8 after 10 cm (4 in), chain off the fabric and continue chaining around stitch tongue for a further 5 – 7 cm (2 – 2¾ in). Go back onto fabric, lower the tension setting to 'balanced' and repeat the procedure to end of marked line.

14. Cut fabric into a square measuring 37 cm (14½ in).

15. *For Block 5 – Lattice-work with dissolving plastic and narrow hem,* use a marking pen to draw two diagonal lines on opposite corners of a piece of plain fabric colour 2. Cut on marked lines.

16. Using the 3 cm-wide (1¼ in-wide) broderie anglaise, sew **lattice-work with dissolving plastic and narrow hem** (see page 15) on cut edges.

17. Cut fabric into a square measuring 37 cm (14½ in).

18. *For Block 6 – Ladder stitch with metallic thread in needle,* use a marking pen to draw four lines at equal distances apart on a piece of plain fabric colour 1 measuring 45 cm x 40 cm (17¾ in x 15¾ in).

19. Using the 6 cm-wide (2¼ in-wide) broderie anglaise, sew **ladder stitch with metallic thread** in needle (see page 12).

20. Cut fabric into a square measuring 37 cm (14½ in).

21. *For Block 7 – Chain stitch with metallic thread,* decorate a piece of plain fabric colour 2 using **chain stitch with metallic thread** (see page 18). To sew the pattern, sew 12 stitches, lift foot and turn fabric at a 45 degree angle, then sew 12 stitches and repeat the lifting of the foot and the turning of the fabric at a 45 degree angle.

22. Cut fabric into a square measuring 37 cm (14½in).

23. *For Block 8 – Flatlocking over ribbon,* draw five lines at equal distances apart on a 45 cm x 40 cm (17¾ in x

DETAIL OF THE CONTINENTAL PILLOWCASE, PATCHWORK DUVET COVER AND TIE-BACK WITH STIFFENED BOWS

15¾ in) piece of plain fabric colour 1. Sew on the 5 cm-wide (2 in-wide) lace and the 3 mm-wide (⅛ in-wide) ribbon, using **flatlocking over ribbon with metallic thread** (see page 12).

24. Cut fabric into a square measuring 37 cm (14½ in).

25. *For Block 9 – Embroidery strings with pottery buttons*, draw four lines at equal distances apart on a piece of plain fabric colour 2 measuring 45 cm x 40 cm (17¾ in x 15¾ in).

26. With WS together, fold the fabric on the marked line and sew **flatlocking with embroidery thread** (see page 12) on the fold, chaining off 10 – 20 cm (4 – 8 in) down the fabric. Repeat the procedure with the remaining three marked lines.

27. Attach pottery buttons to chain.

28. Cut fabric into a square measuring 37 cm (14½ in).

29. *For Block 10 – Flatlocking with embroidery thread*, join the remaining eight strips of plain fabric colour 1 measuring 50 cm x 10 cm (19½ in x 4 in) using **flatlocking with embroidery thread** (see page 12).

30. Turn fabric at a 45 degree angle and cut into a square measuring 37 cm (14½ in).

31. *For Block 11 – Twisted pin-tucks with chain stitch,* decorate a piece of plain fabric colour 2 measuring 50 cm x 40 cm (19½ in x 15¾ in) using **twisted pin-tucks with chain stitch** (see page 18) and the 0.5 – 1 cm-wide (¼ –½ in-wide) ribbon.

32. Cut fabric into a square measuring 37 cm (14½ in).

33. *For Block 12 – Chain stitch with metallic thread,* decorate a piece of plain fabric colour 1 measuring 45 cm x 40 cm (17¾ in x 15¾ in) using **chain stitch with metallic thread** (see page 18). Sew circles very slowly, turning fabric all the while.

34. Cut fabric into a square measuring 37 cm (14½ in).

35. Cut the five 1.5 m-long (1⅔ yd-long) strips of printed fabric in two widthwise. Gather the printed fabric onto the squares for the quilt, using **gathering attachment** (page 9), so that each panel consists of four squares with a gathered strip between them (see Fig. 4).

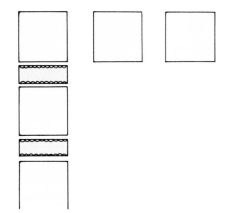

Fig. 4

36. Gather the four 4 m-long (4¼ yd-long) strips to either side of each panel of four squares, using **gathering attachment** (see page 9), to form duvet cover (see Fig. 5).

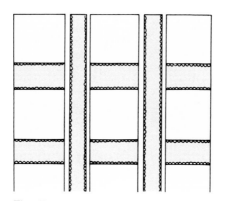

Fig. 5

37. Gather the two 3 m-long (3¼ yd-long) strips to the top and bottom of the duvet cover.

38. Gather all round edges of duvet cover using **gathering attachment**, starting anew at each corner.

39. Sew long edge of front facing to one short edge of duvet cover using three-, four- or five-thread overlocking.

40. Finish raw edge of facing using three-thread overlocking. Fold back 5 cm (2 in) and, using sewing machine, sew with straight stitch.

41. Gather the 9 m (10 yd) broderie anglaise **over embroidery thread** (see page 16).

42. With RS together, pin broderie anglaise to side and bottom edges of front of duvet cover.

43. With RS together, pin plain fabric for back to front of duvet cover.

44. Sew round three sides using three-, four- or five-thread overlocking, starting anew at each corner.

45. Turn cover right side out and insert metal press-studs or poppers to facing on top edge.

PERSONALISED CONTINENTAL PILLOWCASE

The instructions given below are for a continental pillowcase measuring 80 cm (31½ in).

METHOD
1. With RS together, join short edges of fabric for first frill to form a circle, using three-thread overlocking. Repeat with strip for second frill.

2. Finish edges of both frills using **narrow hem with metallic thread** (see page 15).

3. **Gather** both frills **over embroidery thread** (see page 16).

4. Let your daughter draw a picture on the two pieces of white fabric for the front, using the fabric crayons – not too close to the edges, as the seam must still be sewn.

5. Join the printed and illustrated squares, using **flatlocking with embroidery thread** (see page 12).

6. Sew strips of printed fabric to squares using **flatlocking with embroidery thread** (see page 12).

7. Finish one long edge of each piece for the back, using three-thread overlocking.

8. Fold overlocked edges back 1 cm (½ in) and, using sewing machine, sew with straight stitch.

9. With RS together, pin gathered frills to front, positioning the first frill on top of the second frill.

10. Starting anew at each corner, sew on frills, using three-thread overlocking.

11. With RS together, pin backs to front and sew all round using four- or five-thread overlocking, starting anew at each corner. Cut the threads and secure the ends with stitch sealant. Turn pillowcase right side out.

PILLOWCASE IN ONE PIECE

The instructions given below are for a pillowcase measuring 73 cm x 48 cm (28¾ in x 19 in), including a 1 cm (½ in) seam allowance.

> **REQUIREMENTS**
> 1.65 m x 50 cm (1¾ yd x 19½ in)
>   plain fabric
> 50 cm x 12 cm (4¾ in x 4¾ in)
>   insertion lace
> Floss
> Polyester cotton thread to
>   match fabric
> Marking pen
> Stitch sealant (see page 19)

METHOD

1. Finish both short edges of plain fabric using three-thread overlocking.

2. Fold one short edge back 2 cm (¾ in) and, using sewing machine and straight stitch, sew hem.

3. Fold back 15 cm (6 in) along other short edge and press.

4. Using marking pen, draw a line 15 cm (6 in) from the folded edge and cut.

5. With WS together, sew the insertion lace to the fabric using **three-thread flatlocking with floss** (see page 11 and Fig. 6).

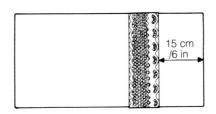

Fig. 6

6. With RS together, fold the 15 cm (6 in) folded edge over the 2 cm (¾ in) hemmed edge (see Fig. 7).

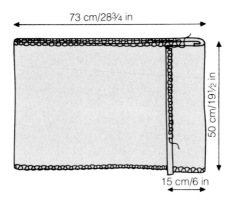

73 cm/28¾ in

50 cm/19½ in

15 cm/6 in

Fig. 7

7. Pin, then sew the side seams using four- or five-thread overlocking.

8. Seal ends with stitch sealant.

9. Turn pillowcase right side out.

NIGHT FRILL

The instructions given are for a night frill for a bed measuring 200 cm x 150 cm (79 in x 59 in).

CALCULATING THE AMOUNT OF FABRIC REQUIRED

To calculate the length of the frill, measure the width of the bed and twice the length of the bed (see Fig. 8) and multiply by 2.

To calculate the width of the frill, measure from the edge of the base of the bed to the floor and add on a 1 cm (½ in) hem allowance. For the centre piece, measure the width and the length of the base of the bed and add on a 1 cm (½ in) seam allowance all round.

15 cm /6 in

Fig. 8

> **REQUIREMENTS**
> 2 m x 150 cm (2¼ yd x 59 in)
>   white fabric for centre piece
> 11 m x 32 cm-wide (12 yd x
>   12½ in-wide) plain or printed
>   fabric for frill
> Metallic thread
> Polyester cotton thread to
>   match fabric
> Stitch sealant (see page 19)

METHOD

1. Fold one short edge of centre piece back 1 cm (½ in) and, using sewing machine, sew with straight stitch.

2. If necessary, join strips of fabric for frill, using three-thread overlocking, to obtain the required length.

3. Finish the edge of the fabric for the frill, using **narrow hem with metallic thread** (see page 15).

4. Fold short edges of fabric for frill back 1 cm (½ in) and, using sewing machine, sew with straight stitch.

5. Join frill to centre piece using **gathering attachment** (see page 9).

> **NOTE:** If you do not have a gathering plate, or cannot fit one onto your overlocker, **gather** frill **over embroidery thread** (see page 16).

SUPPLIERS' ADDRESSES

THE FOUR POSTER
(Stockists of fabric and matching
accessories)
Head Office
P O Box 83, Southfield,
Cape Town 7880
Tel: (021) 72 7760
Branches
Cavendish Square, Claremont
Tel: (021) 683 5689 or 61 9636
Sandton City, Johannesburg
Tel: (011) 883 4045/783 3233
Tygervalley, Cape Town
Tel: (021) 948 9255

ELNA
(Stockists of ELNA sewing machines
and overlockers)
Main Centres
Johannesburg – P O Box 318,
Randburg 2125
Tel: (011) 792 4900
Cape Town – P O Box 2043,
Bellville 7535
Tel: (021) 945 1113

Durban – P O Box 165,
Durban 4001
Aliwal Street
Tel (031) 304 4304
Umgeni Road
Tel (031) 23 8756 or 303 2603

PICK 'N PAY
(Stockists of FINESSE overlockers)
Head Office
P O Box 23087,
Claremont,
Cape Town 7735
Tel: (021) 683 2140

**SERALON (a member of the ACA
Group)**
(Stockists of threads and crochet
cotton)
Cape – P O Box 100,
Brackenfell 7560
Tel: (021) 981 1133
Transvaal – P O Box 4246,
Johannesburg 2000
Tel: (011) 337 2531

**LAMÉ NEEDLEWORK AND CRAFTS
SCHOOL**
(Stockists of Madeira metallic thread,
dissolving plastic, Fray Check,
batting, placemat batting,
dressmaker's tracing paper, polyester
filling, Stiffy [PVA Adhesive] and
Modge Podge [Acrylic glaze])
9 Old Paarl Road, Bellville 7530
Tel: (021) 948 8892

VYNIDE
(Stockists of vynide plastics [PVC])
Somerset West
Tel: (024) 51 7105

CNA
(Stockists of fabric crayons)
Main Branches
Bloemfontein – (051) 48 1731/2
Cape Town – (021) 54 1261
Durban – (031) 465 1875
East London – (0431) 26 304
Johannesburg – (011) 493 3200
Port Elizabeth – (041) 55 9006/8

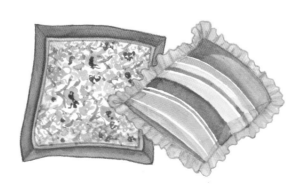

INDEX